This Book belongs to :

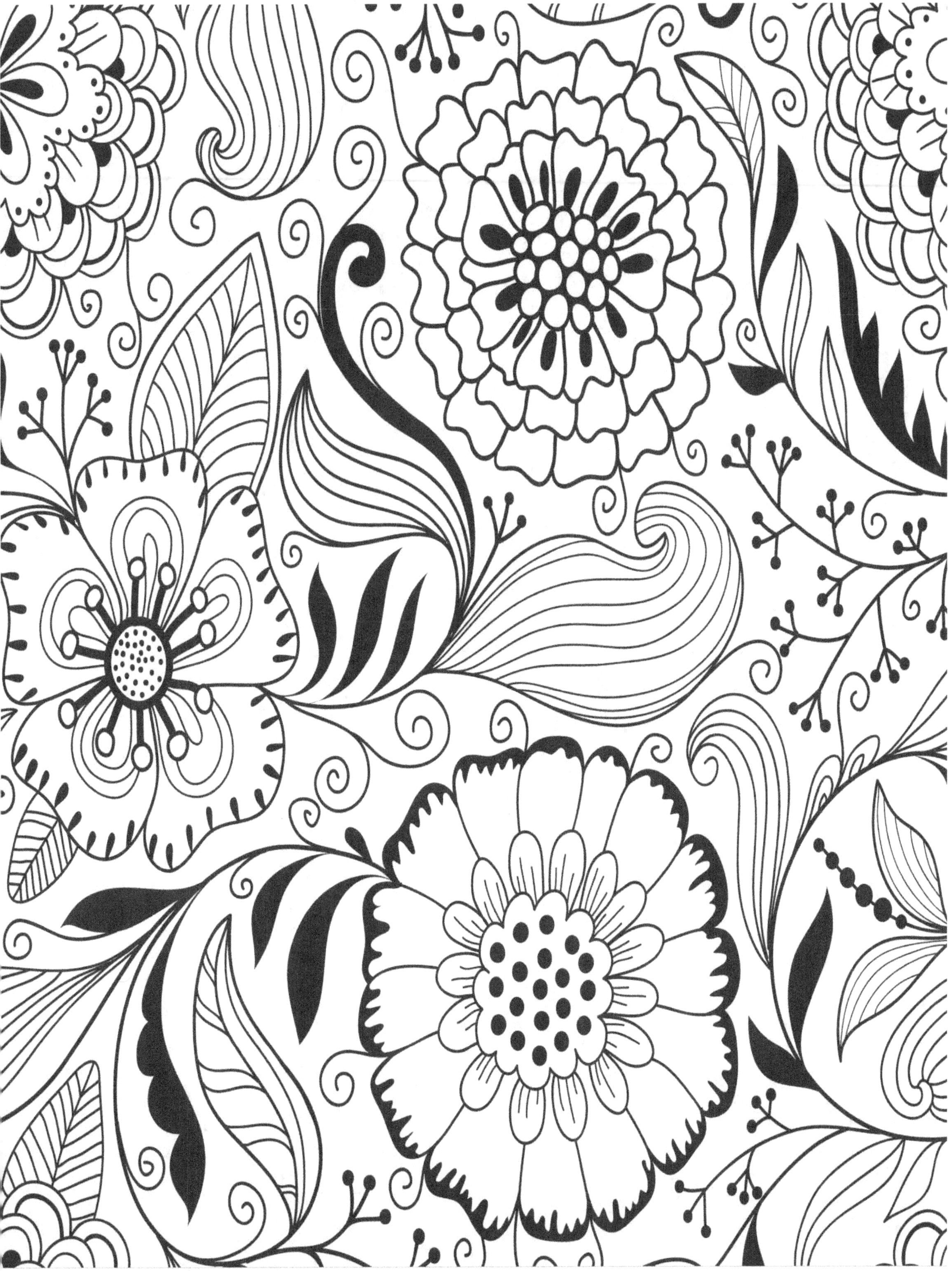

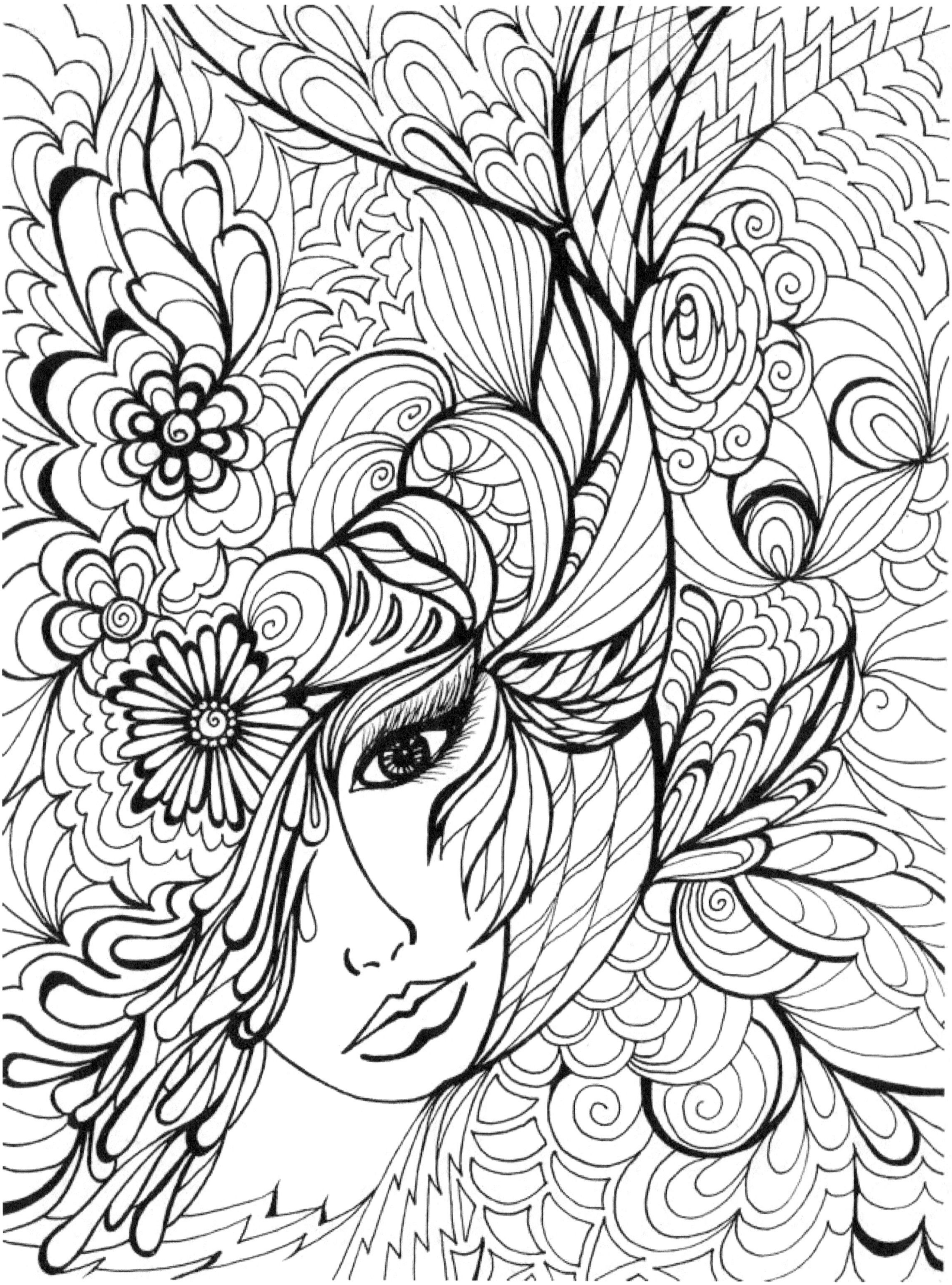

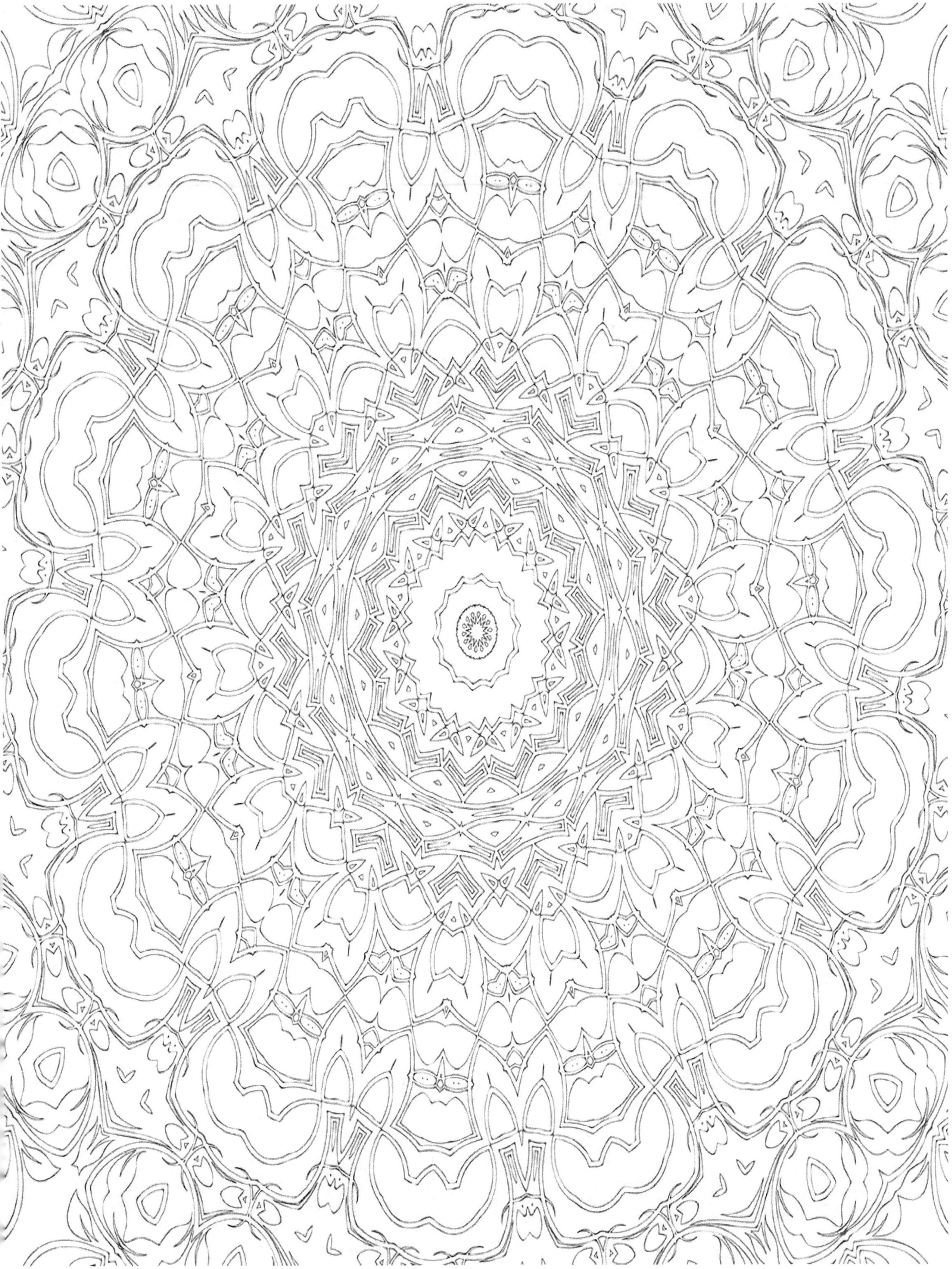

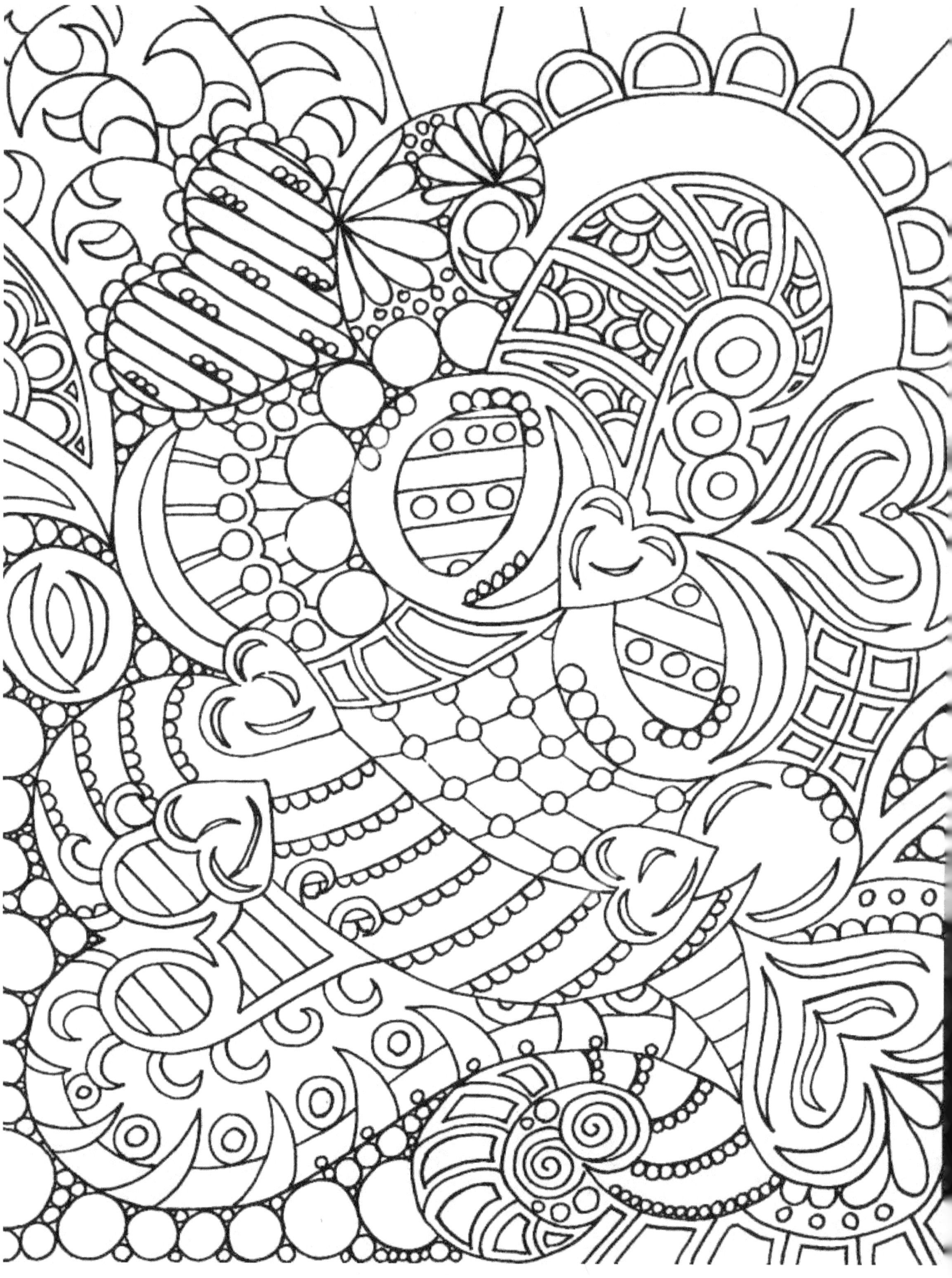

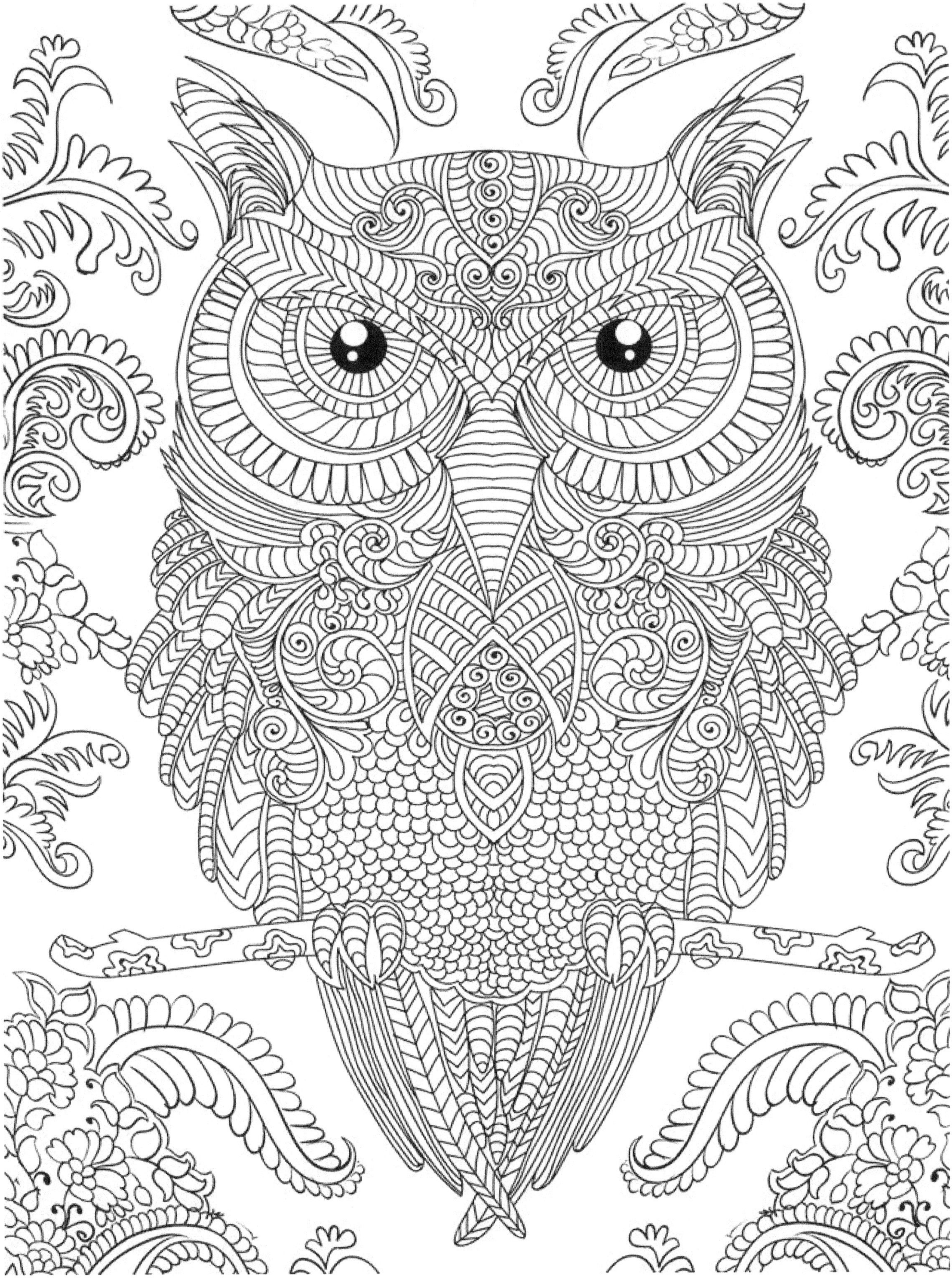

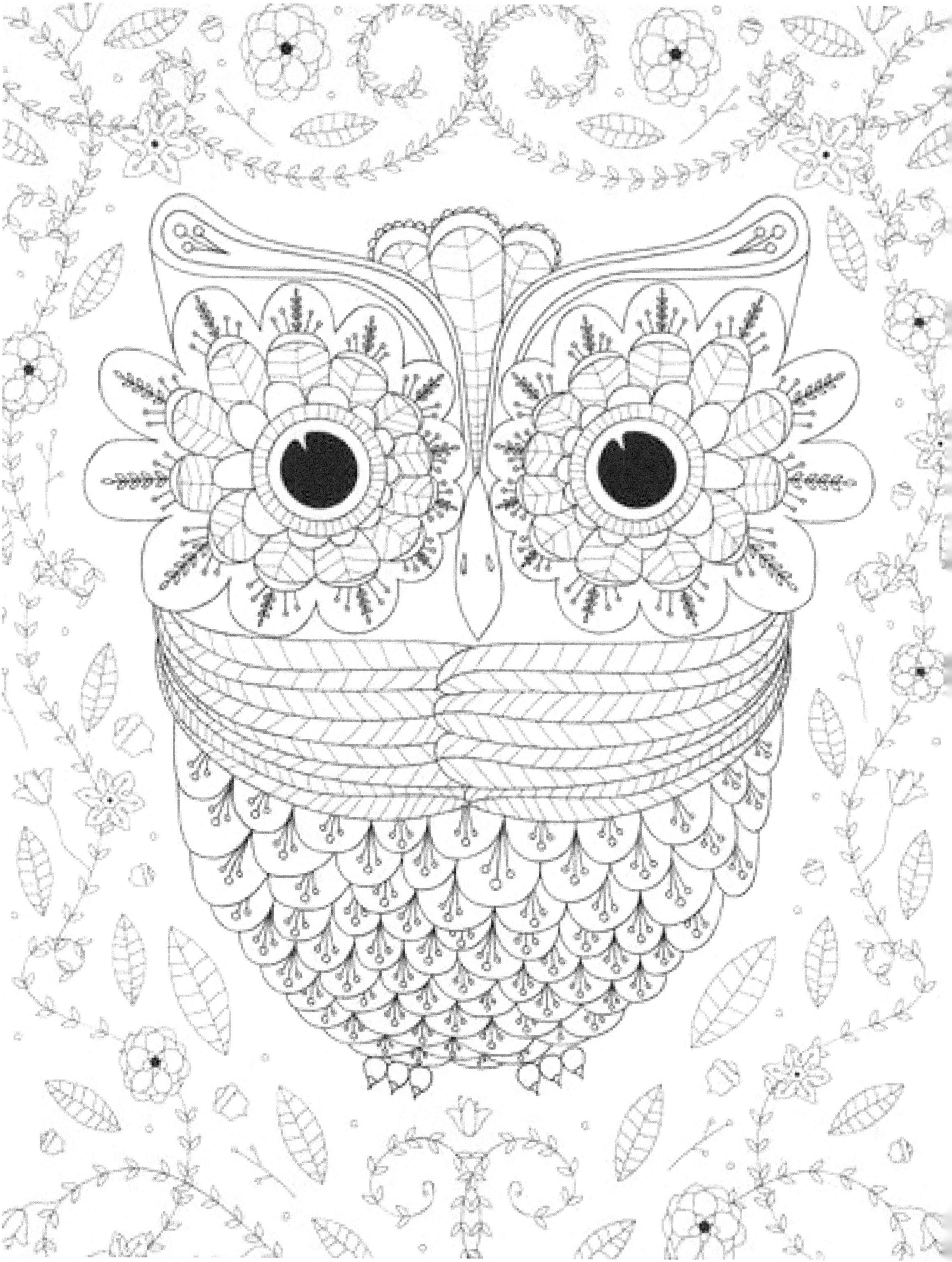

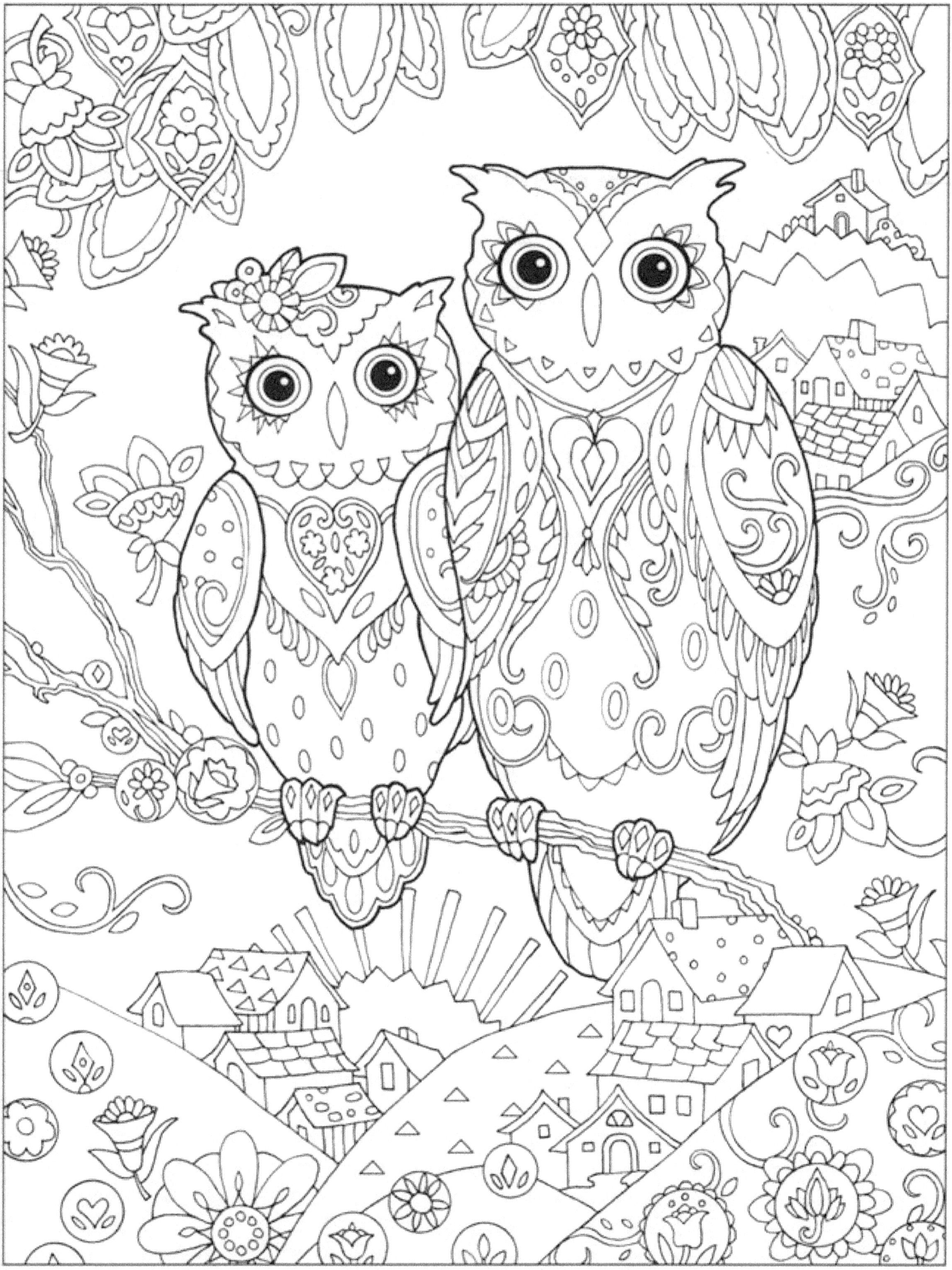

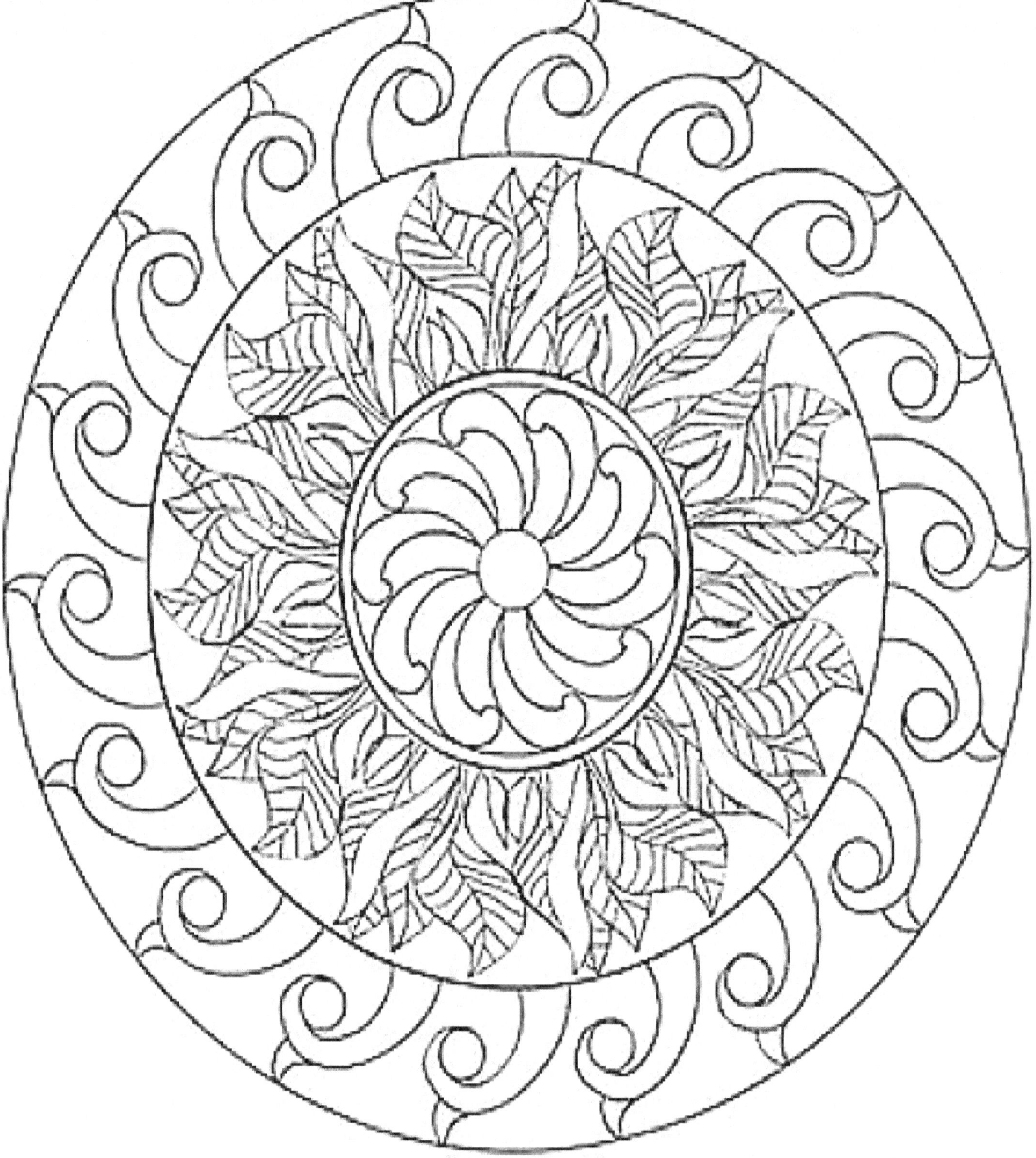

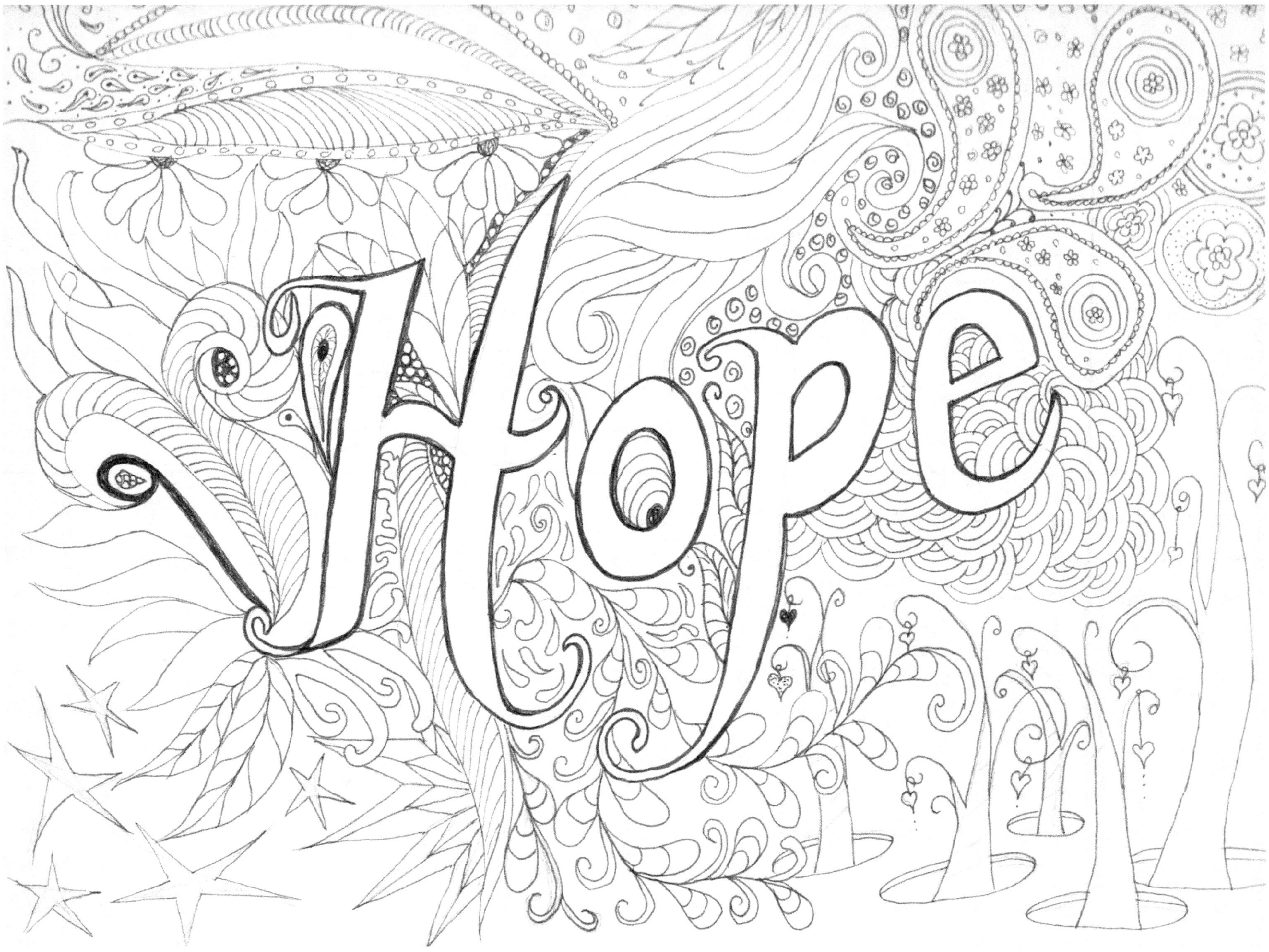
Hope

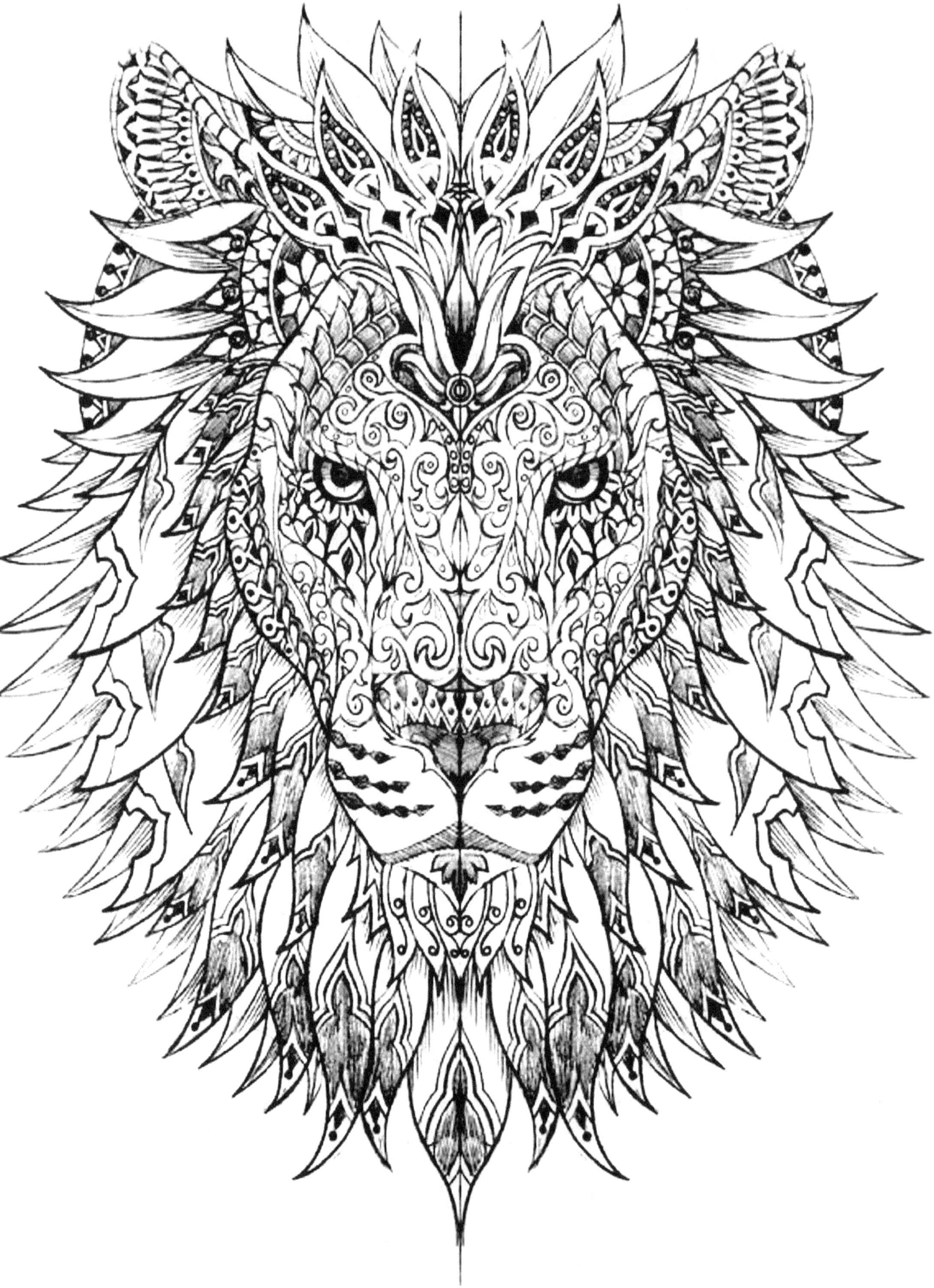

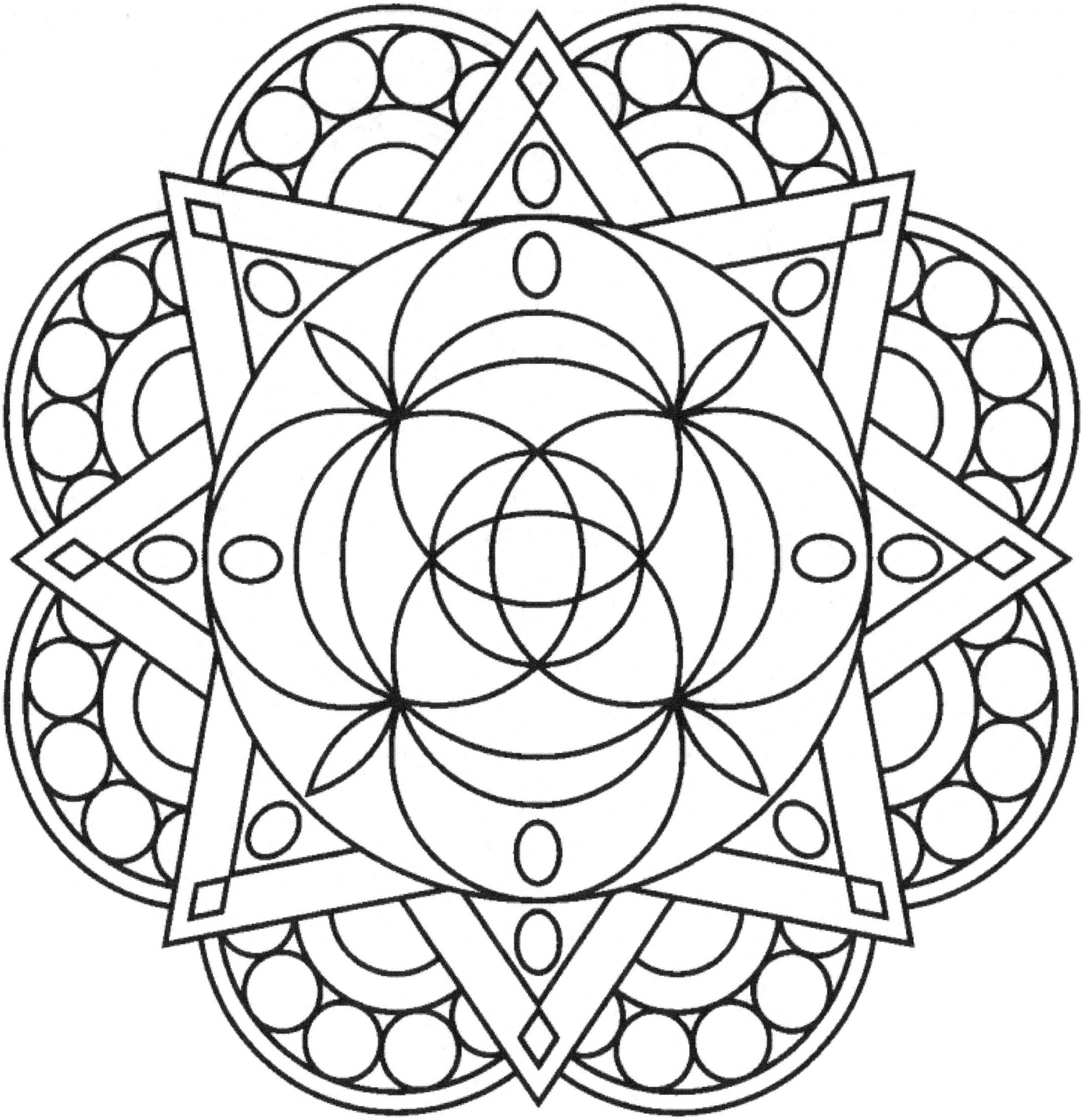

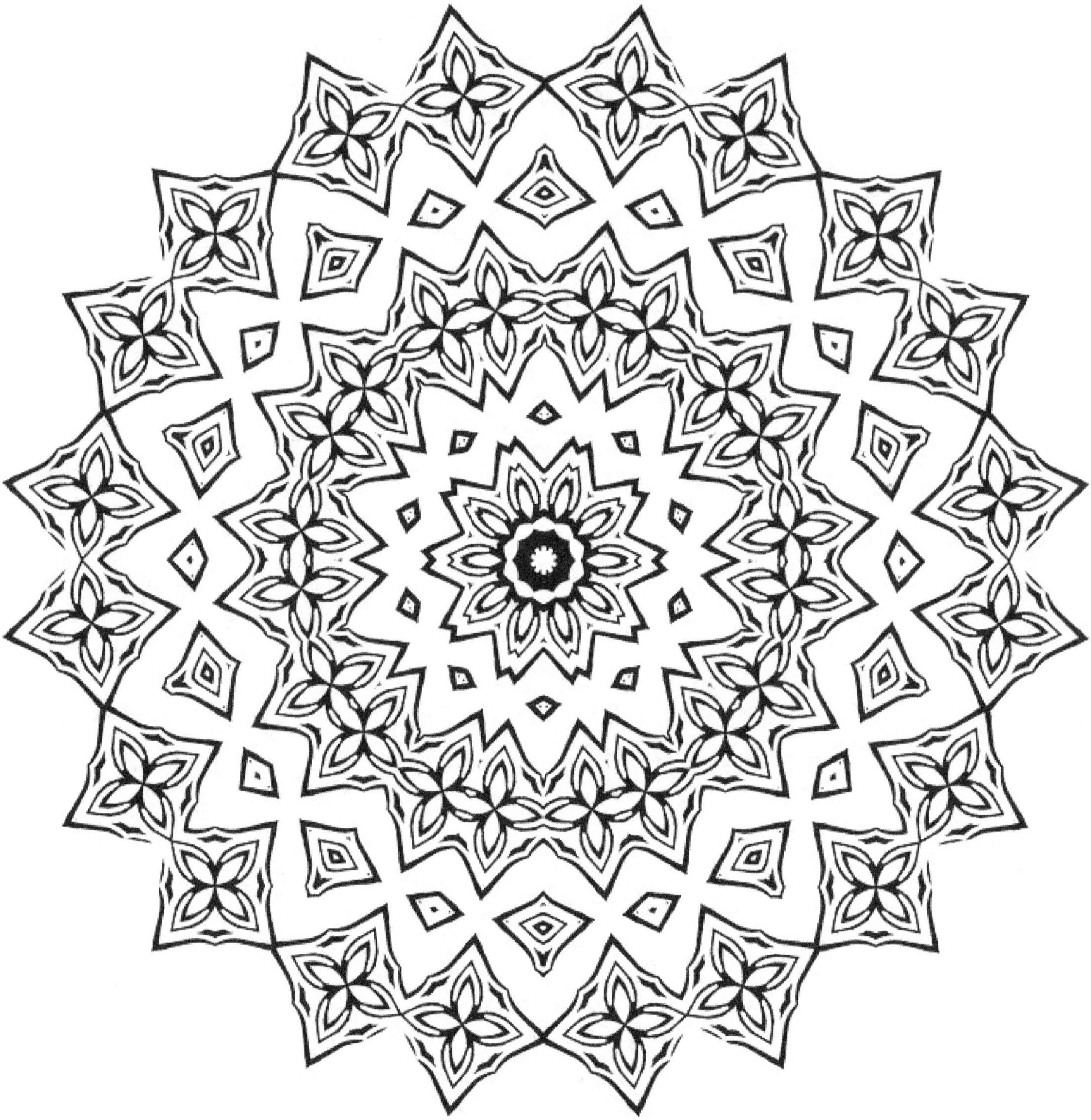

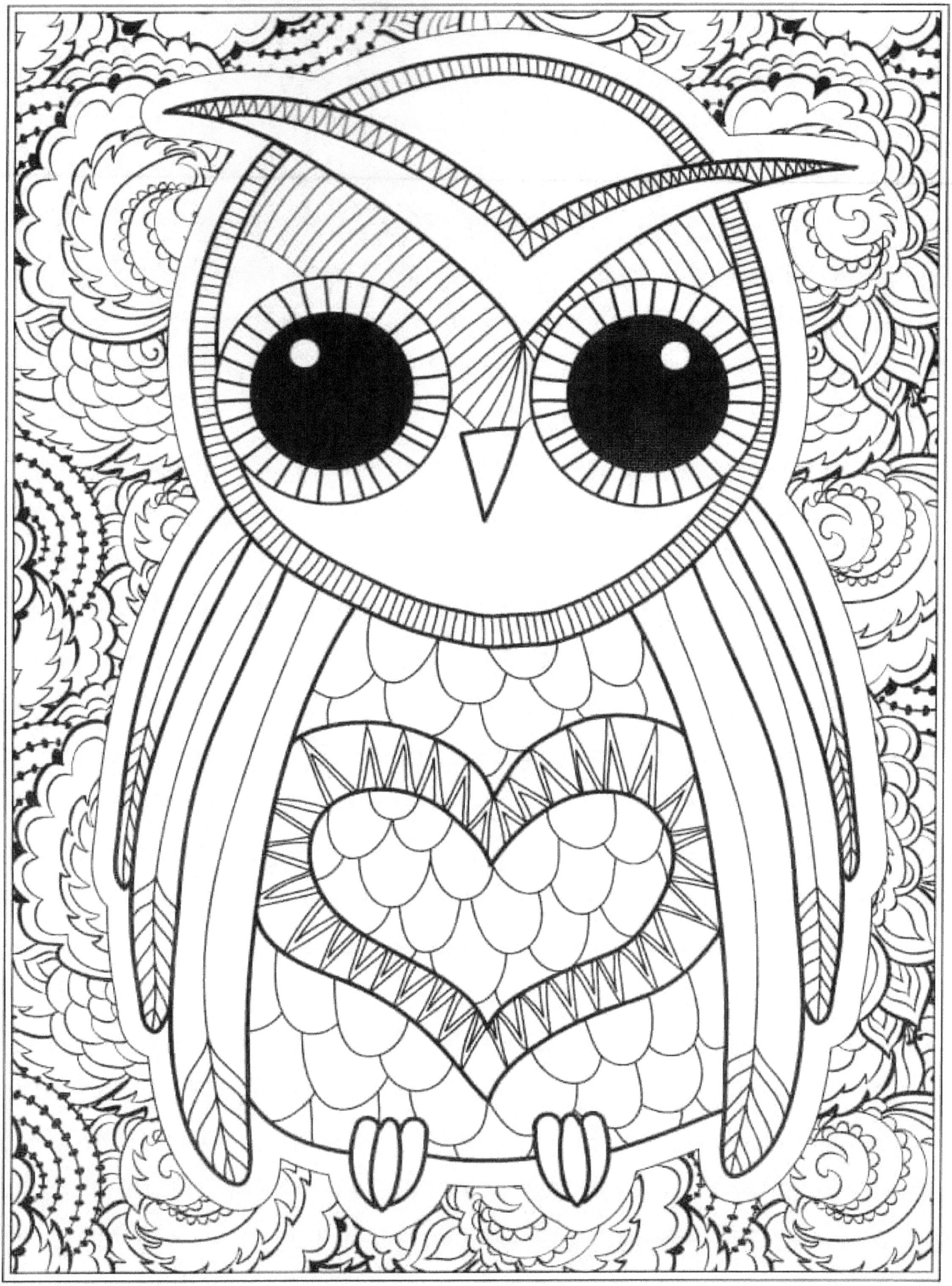

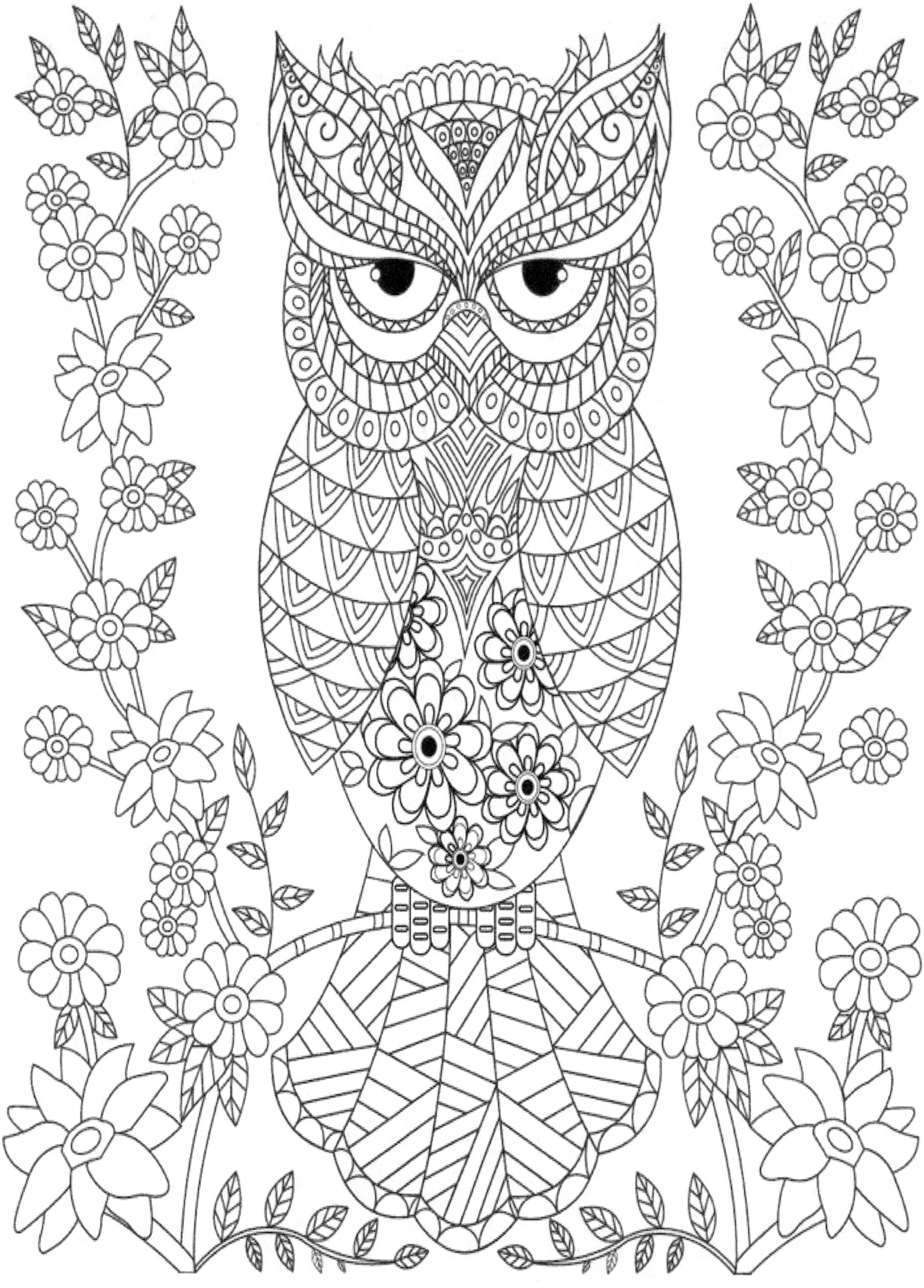

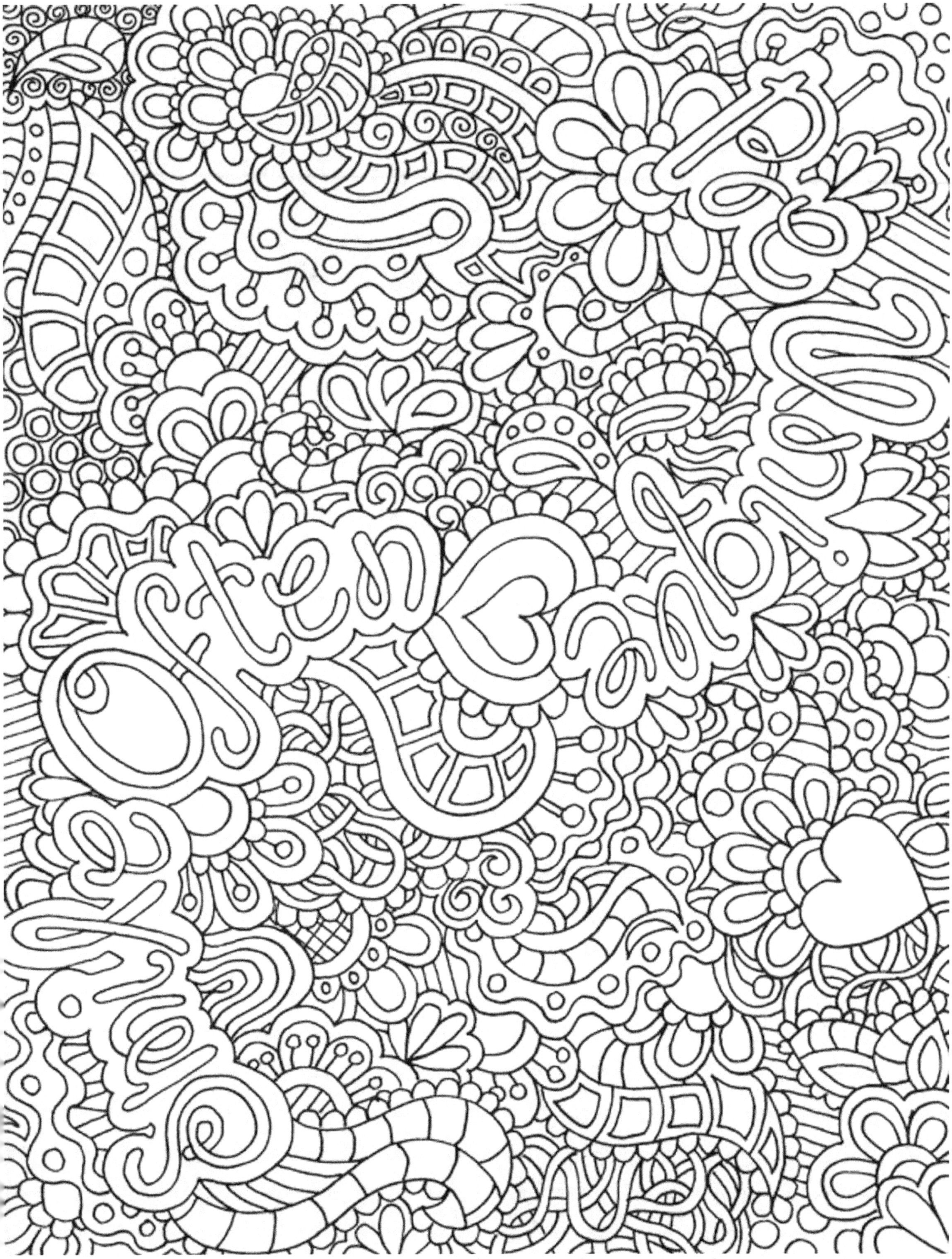
Often

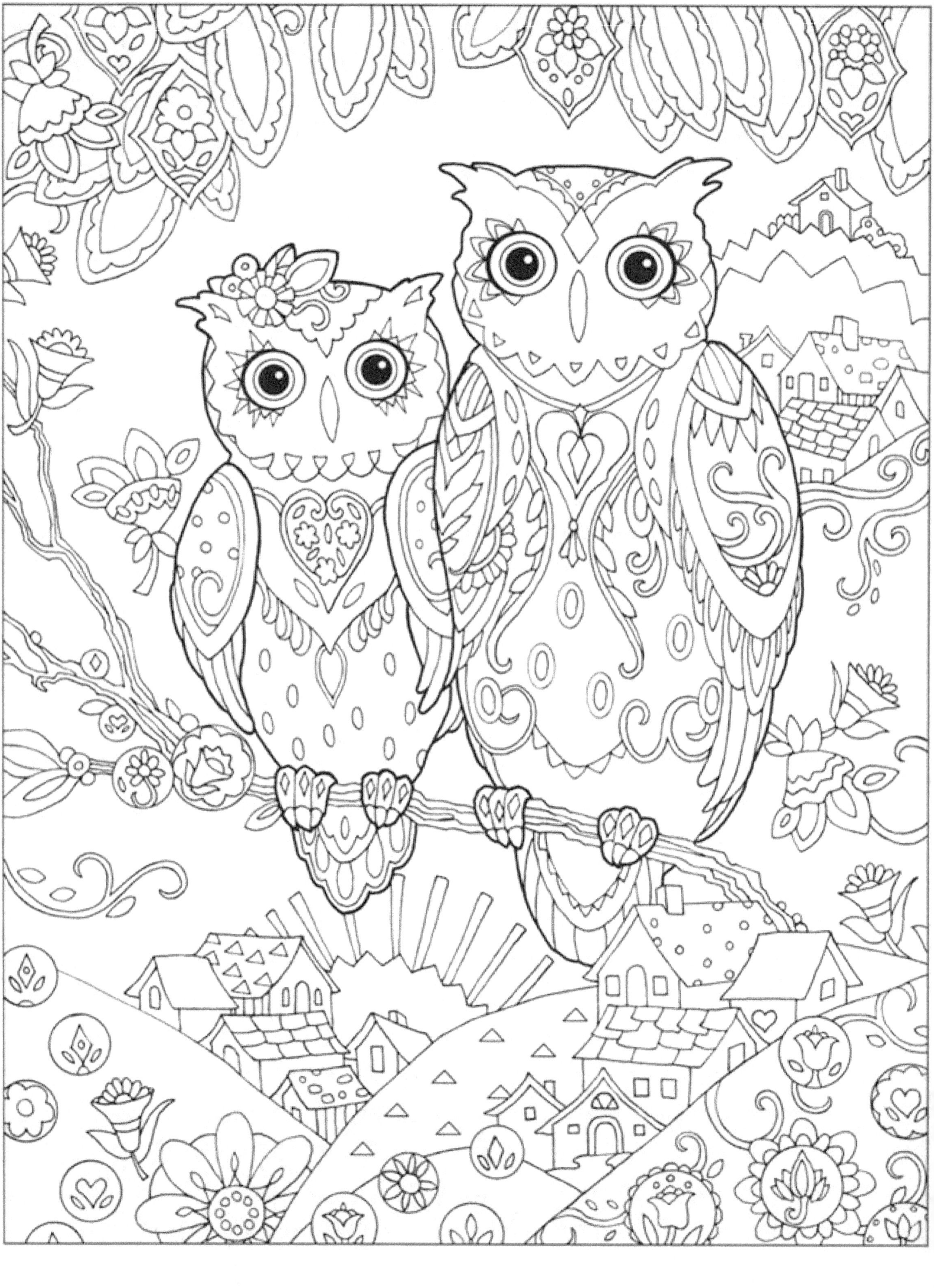

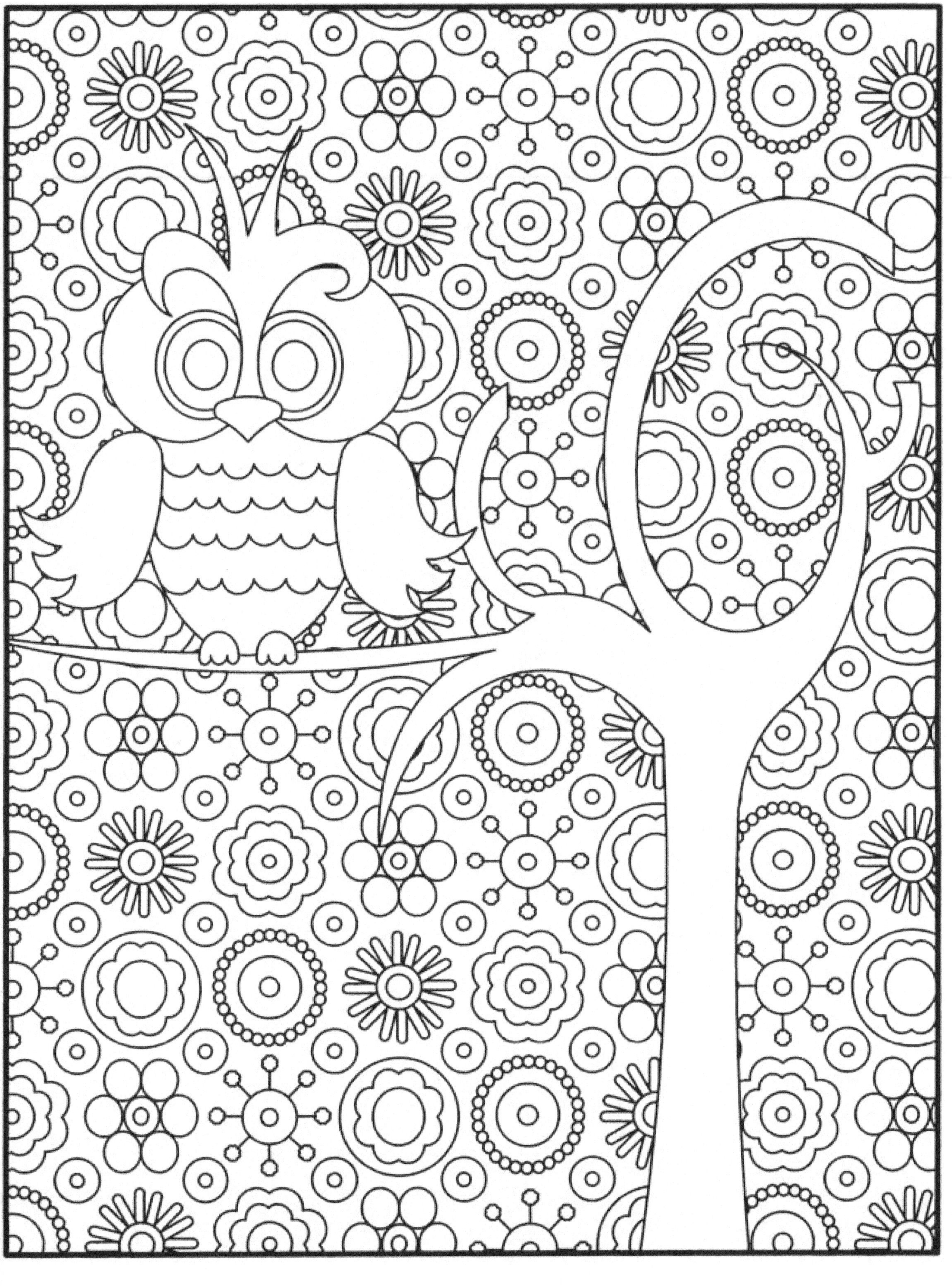

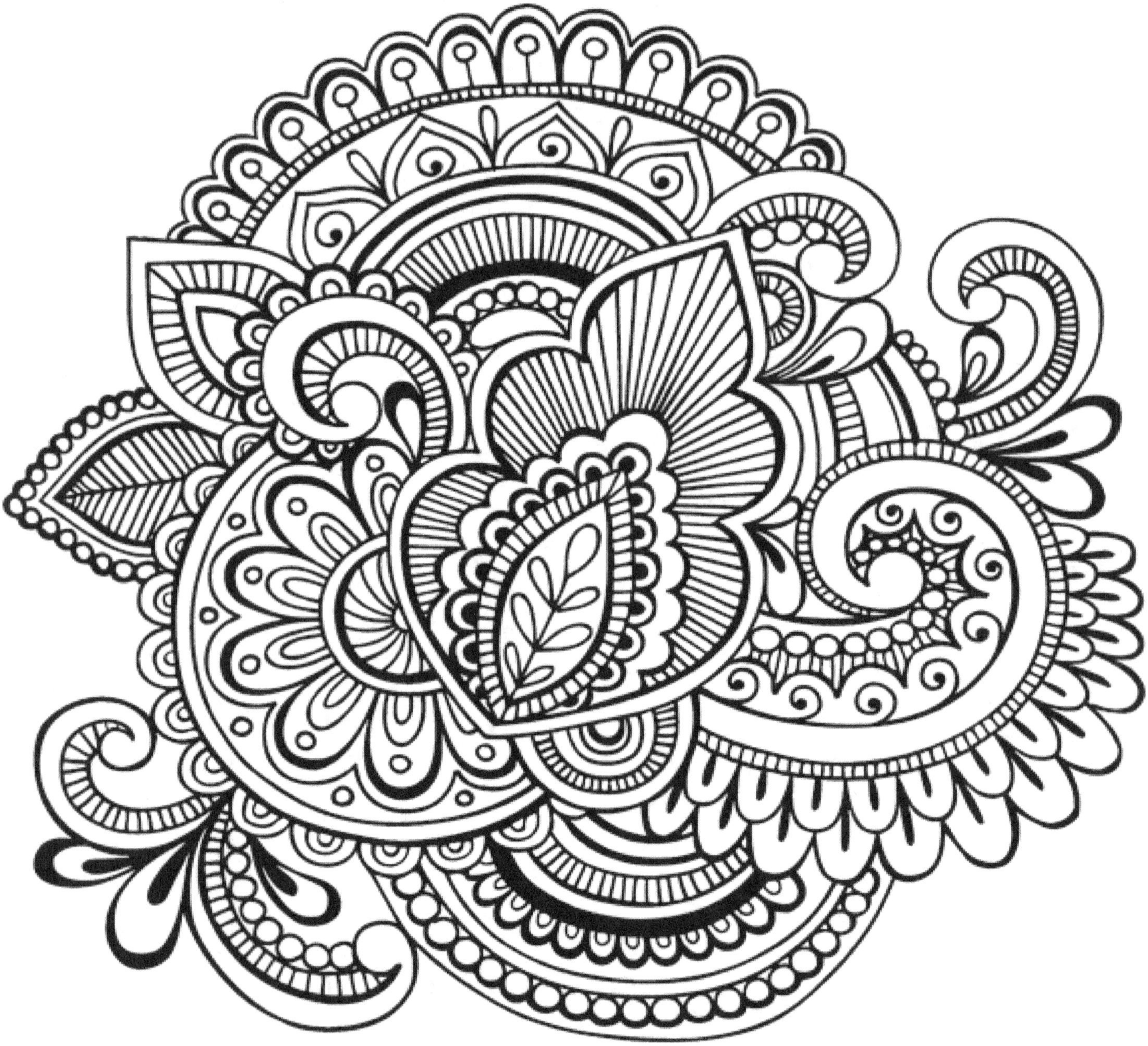

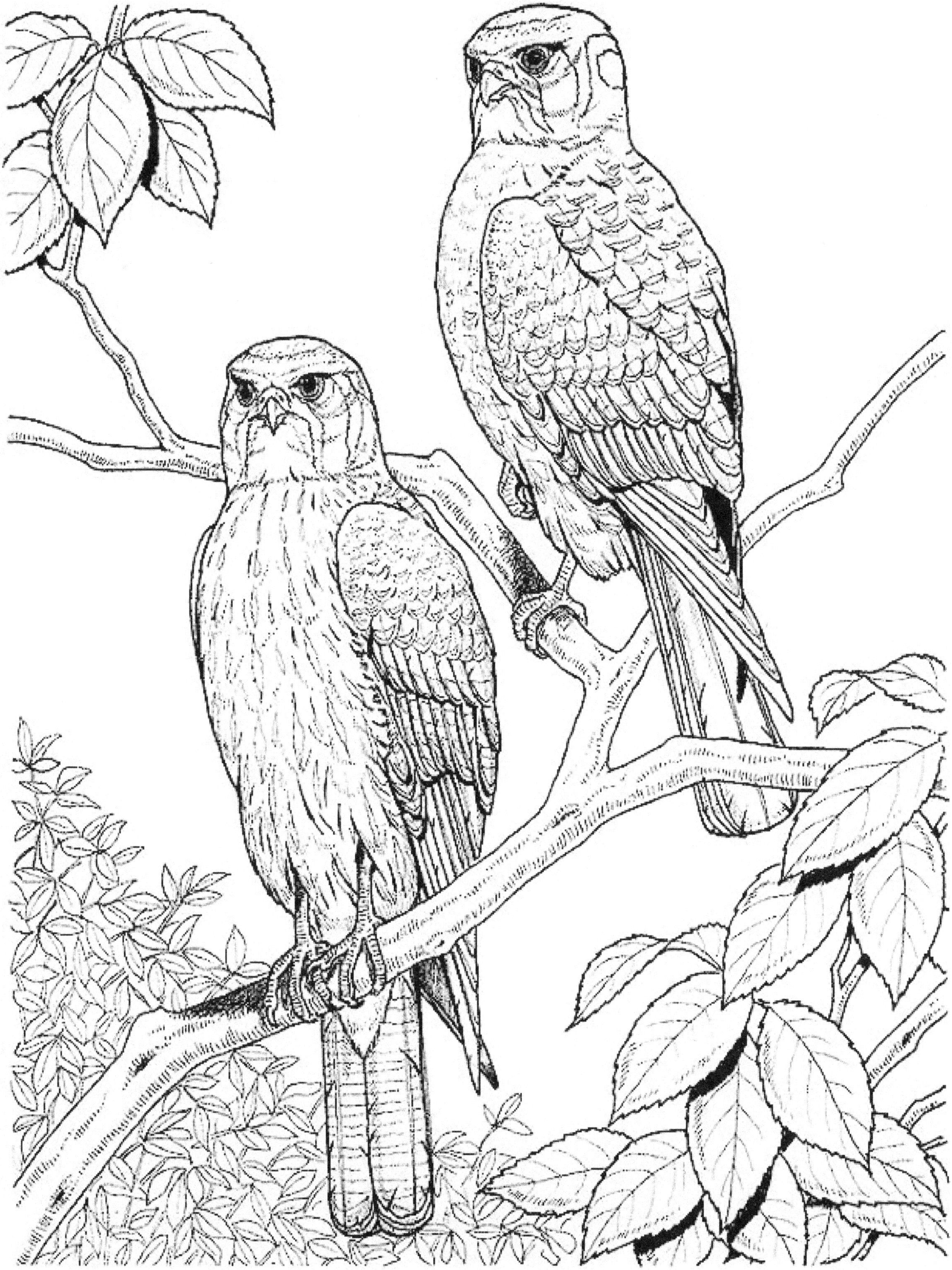

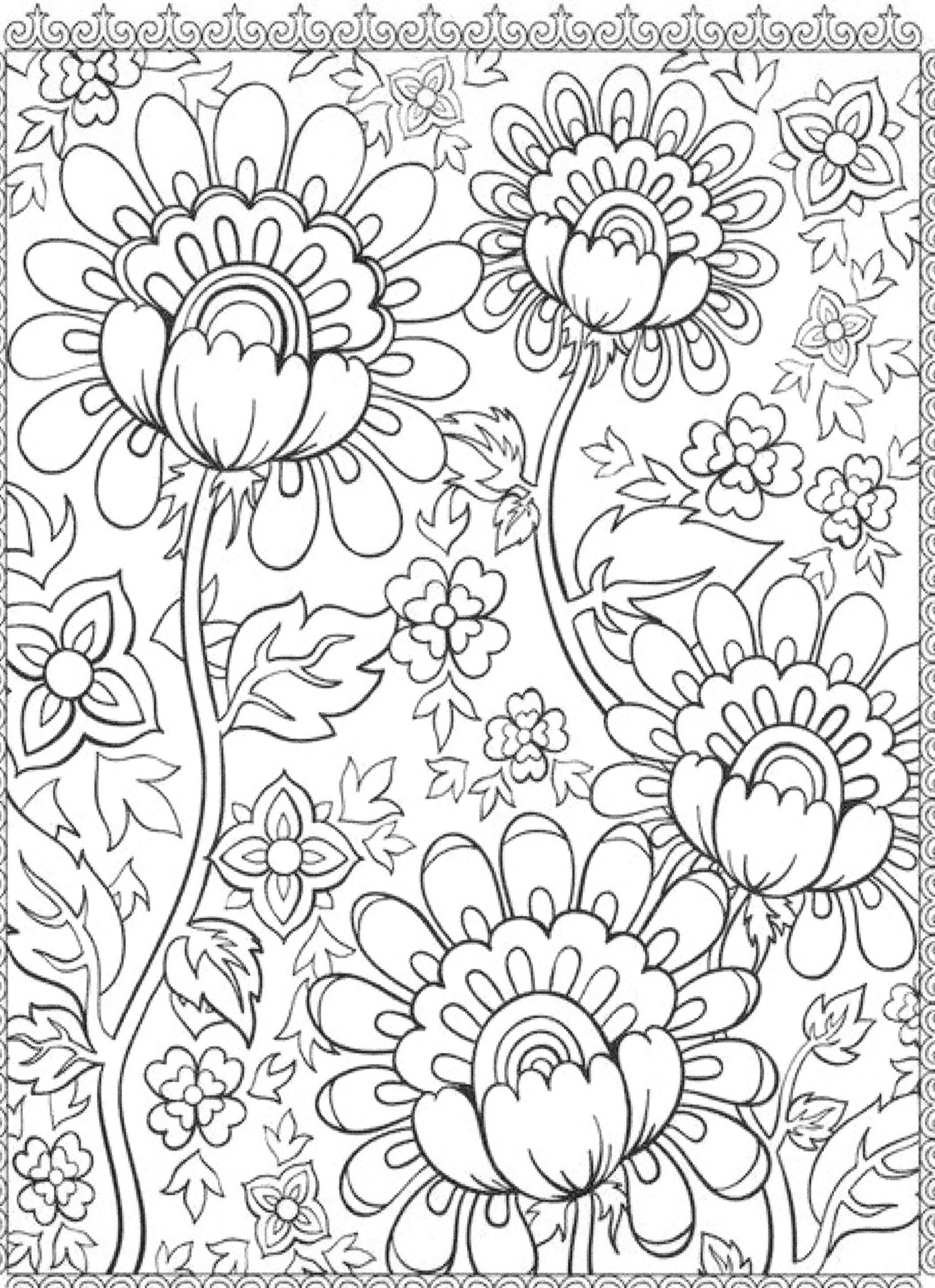

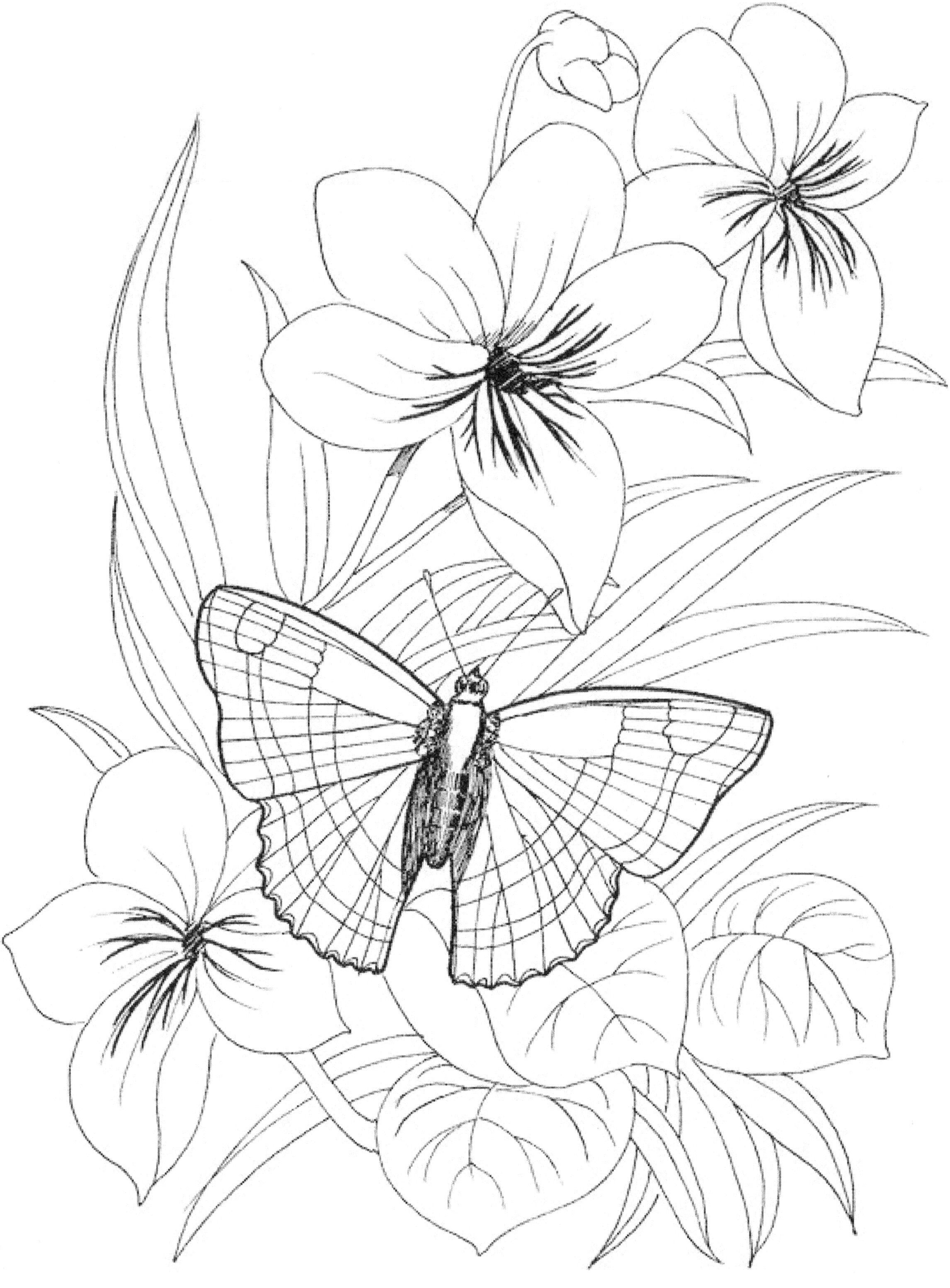

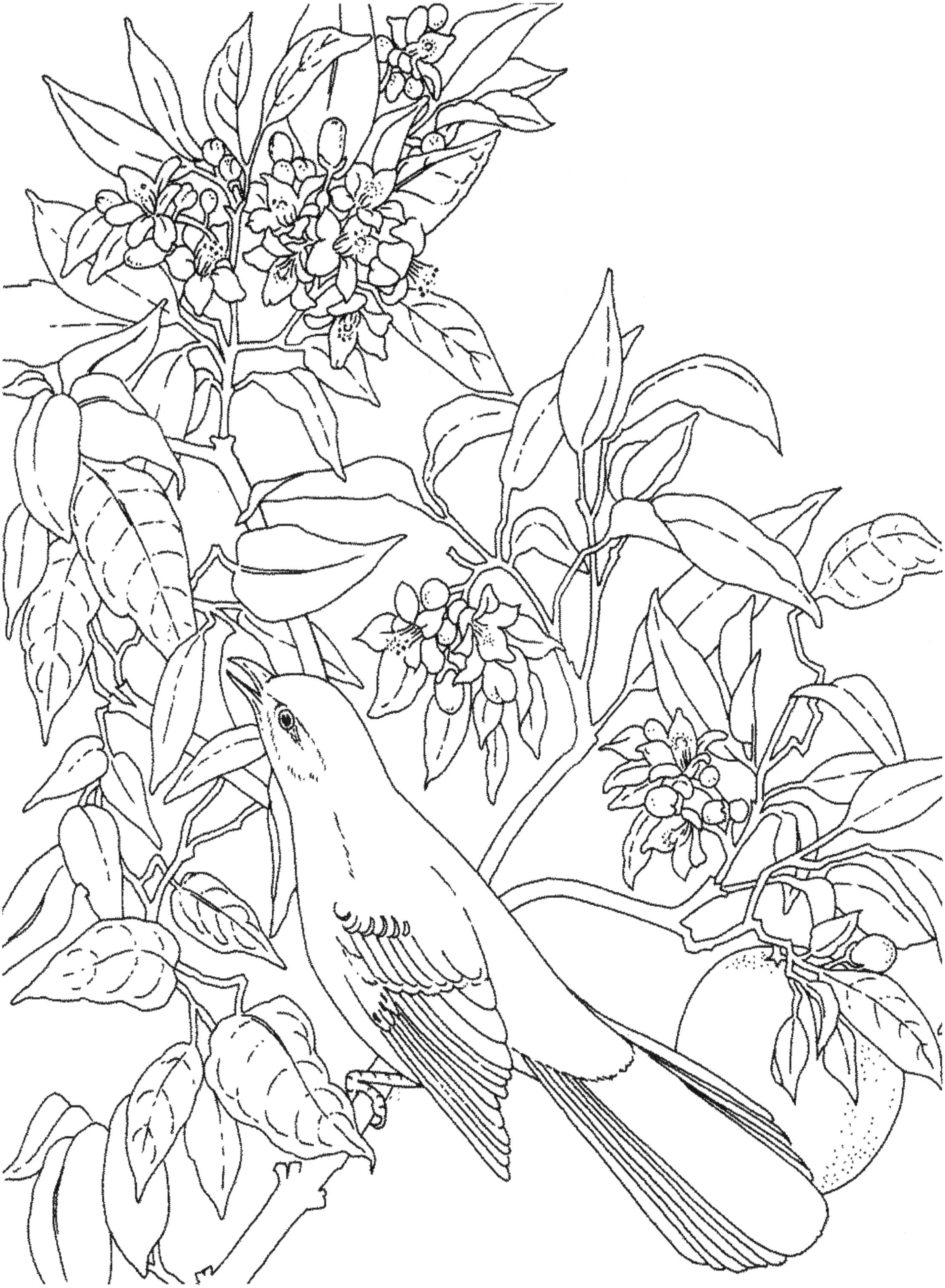

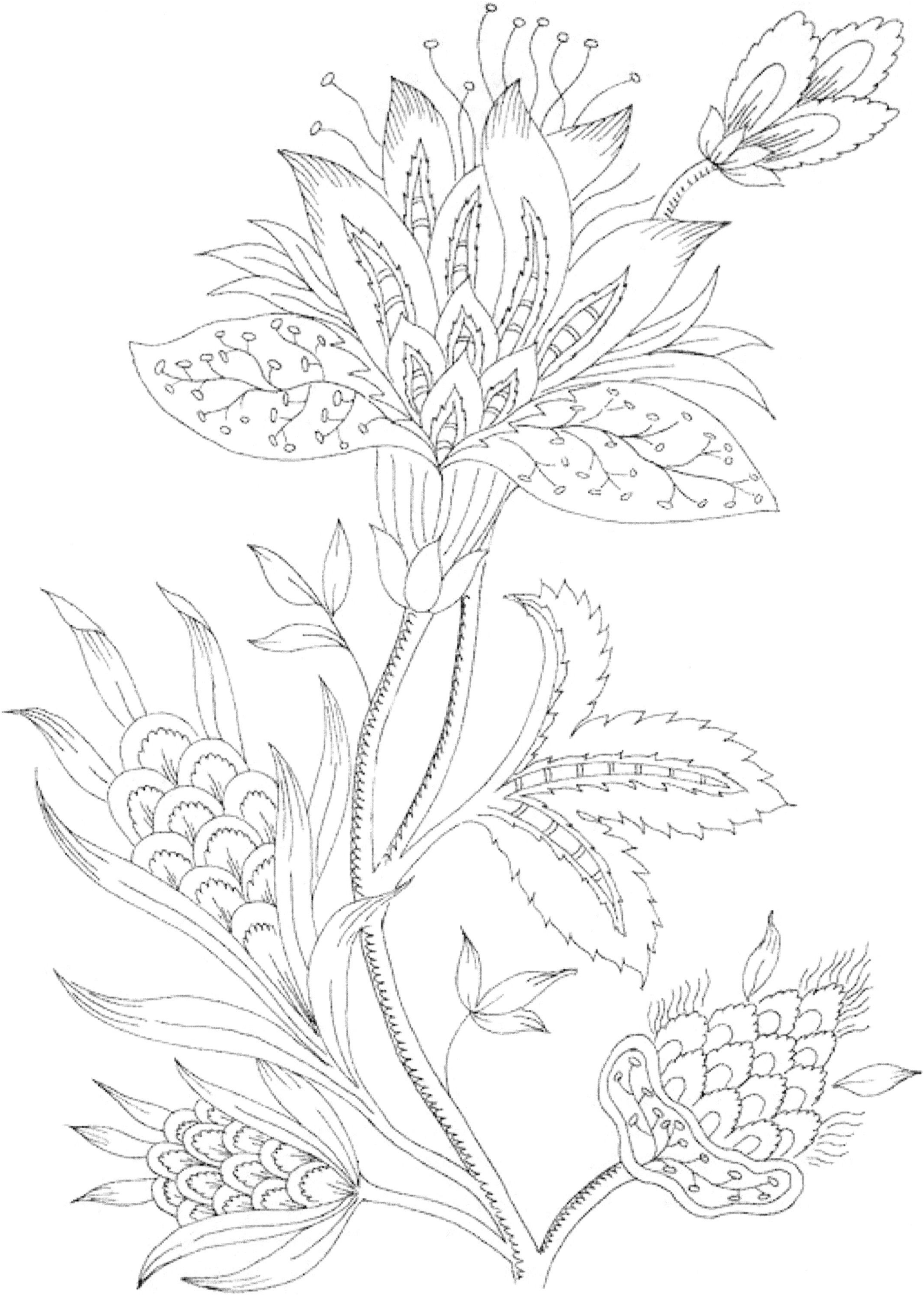

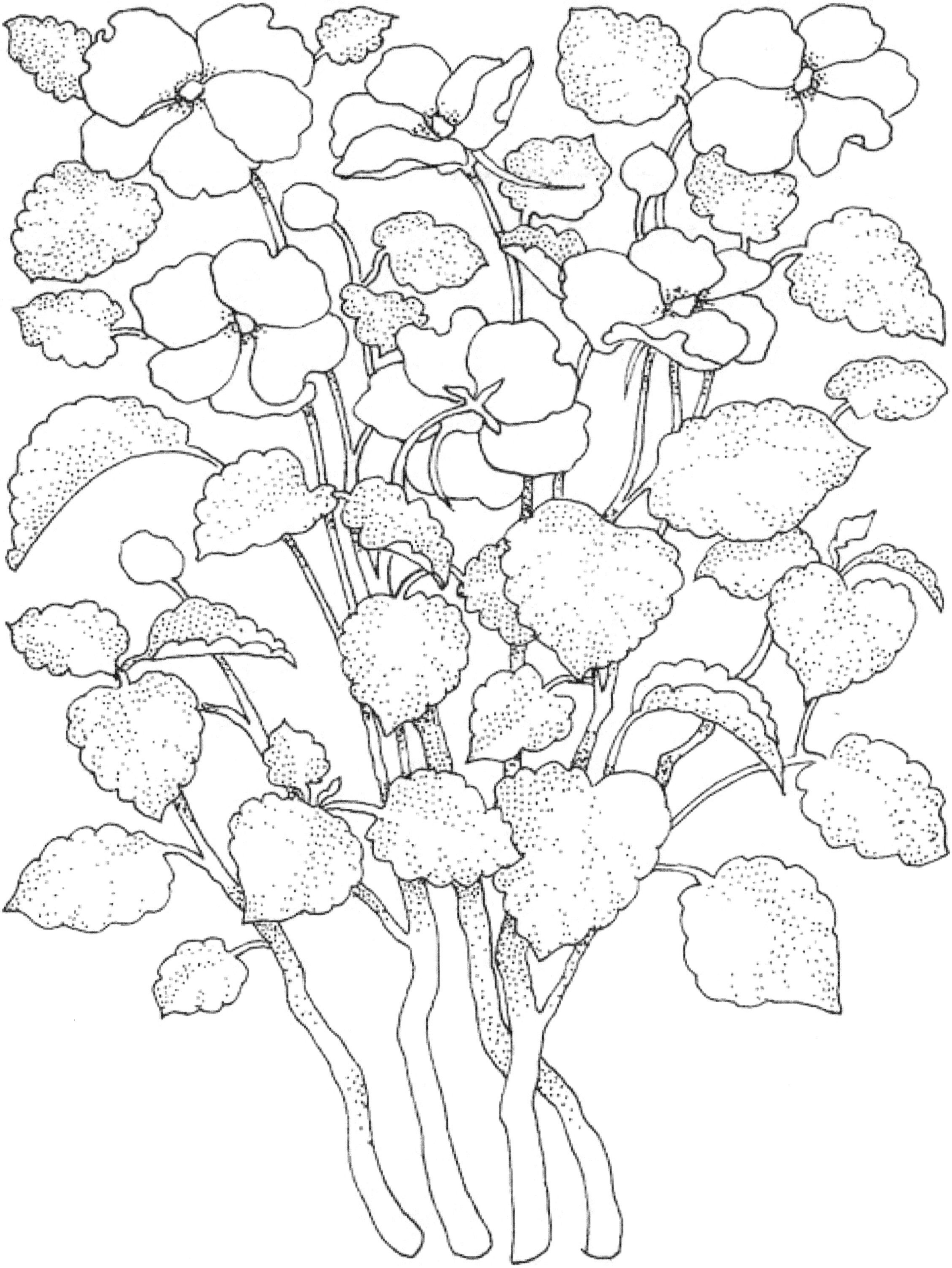

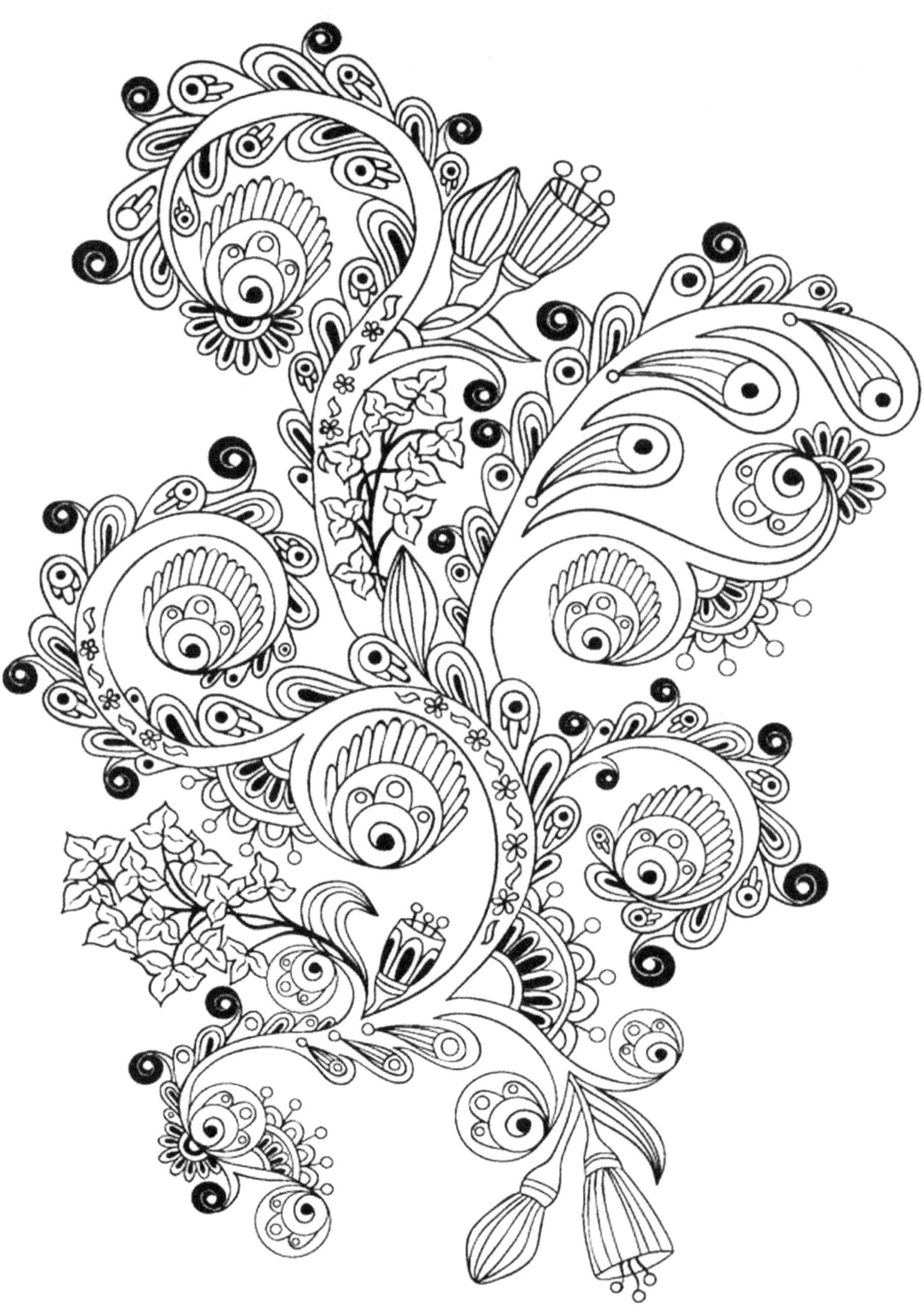

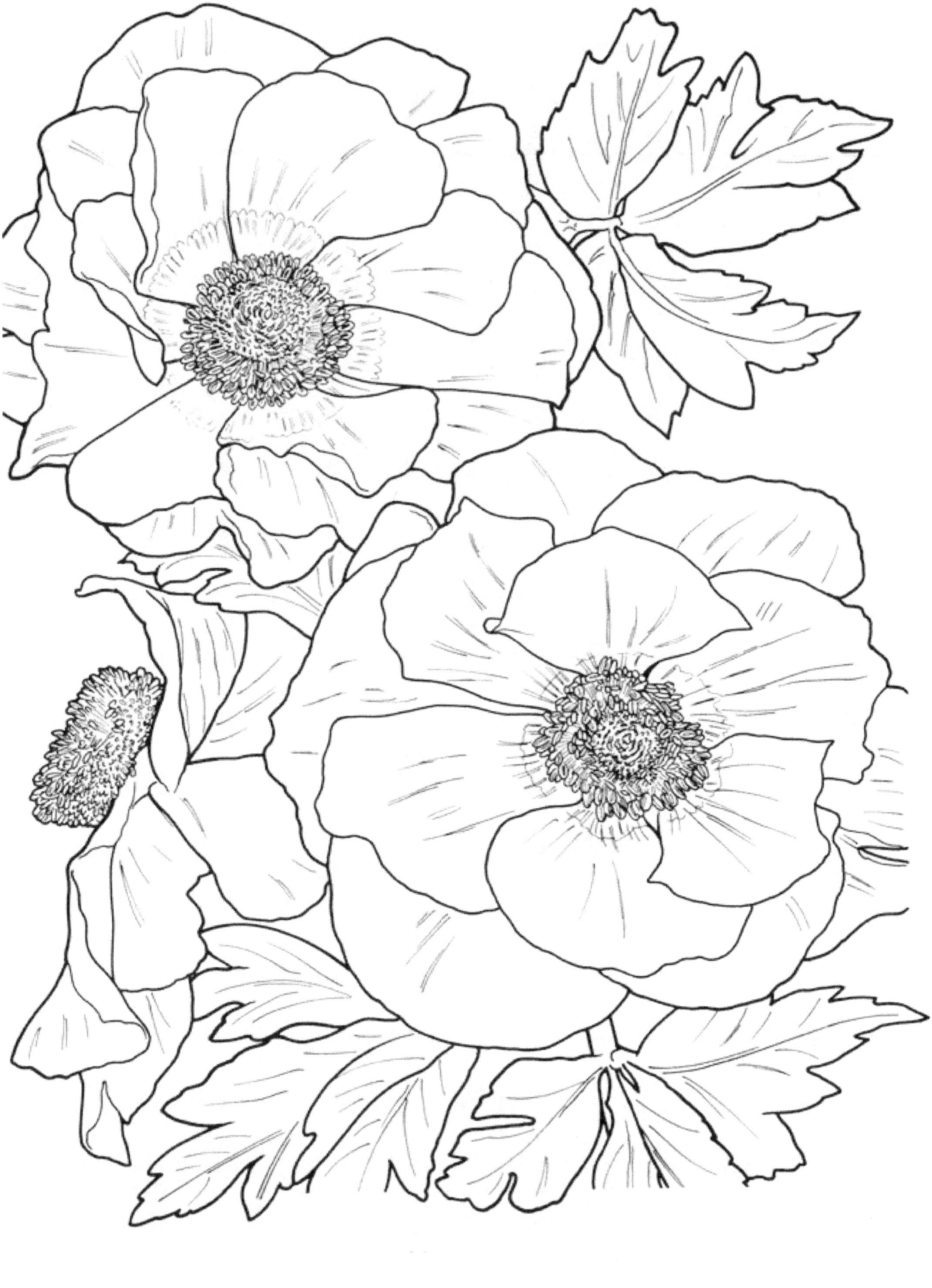

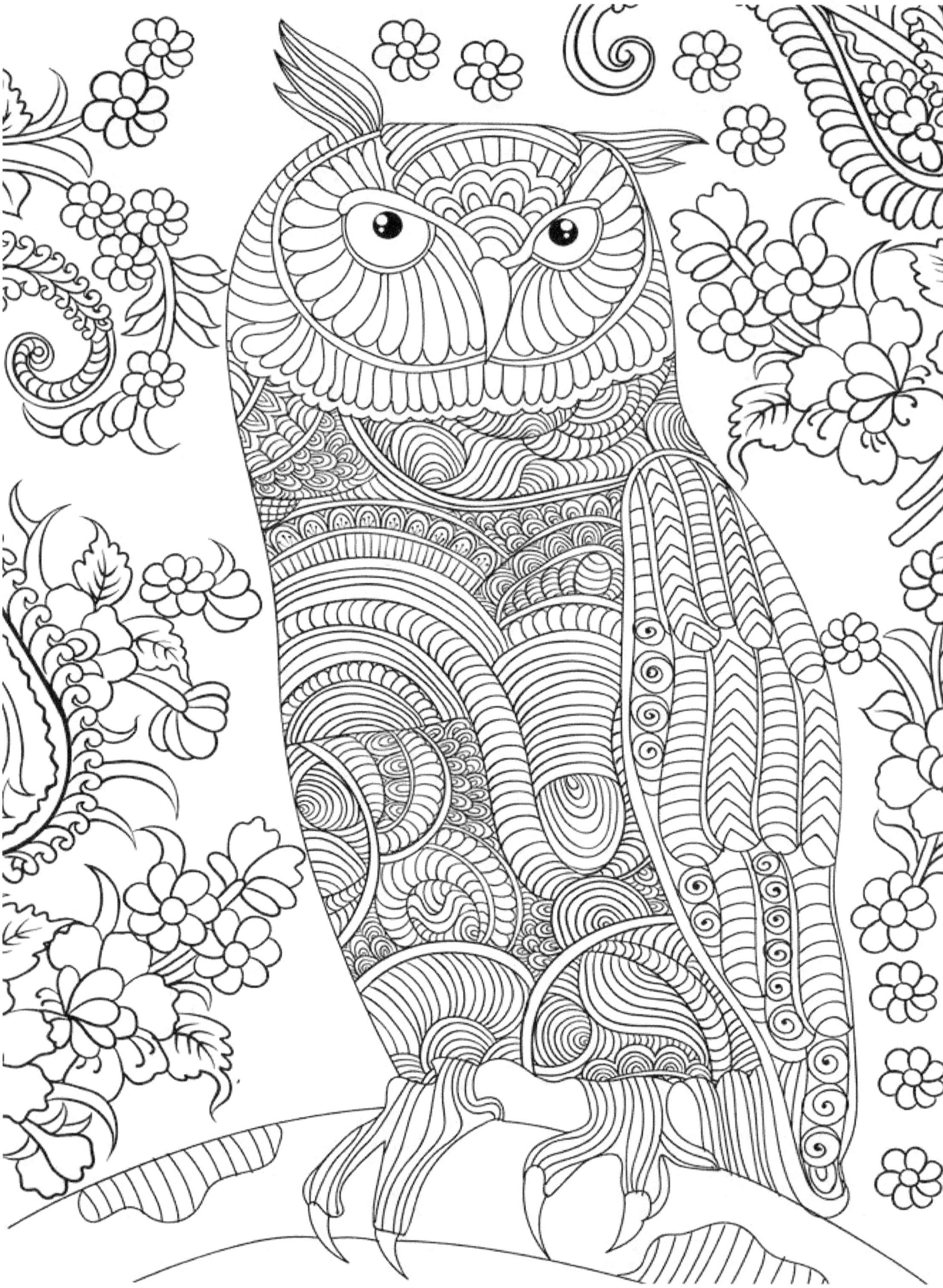

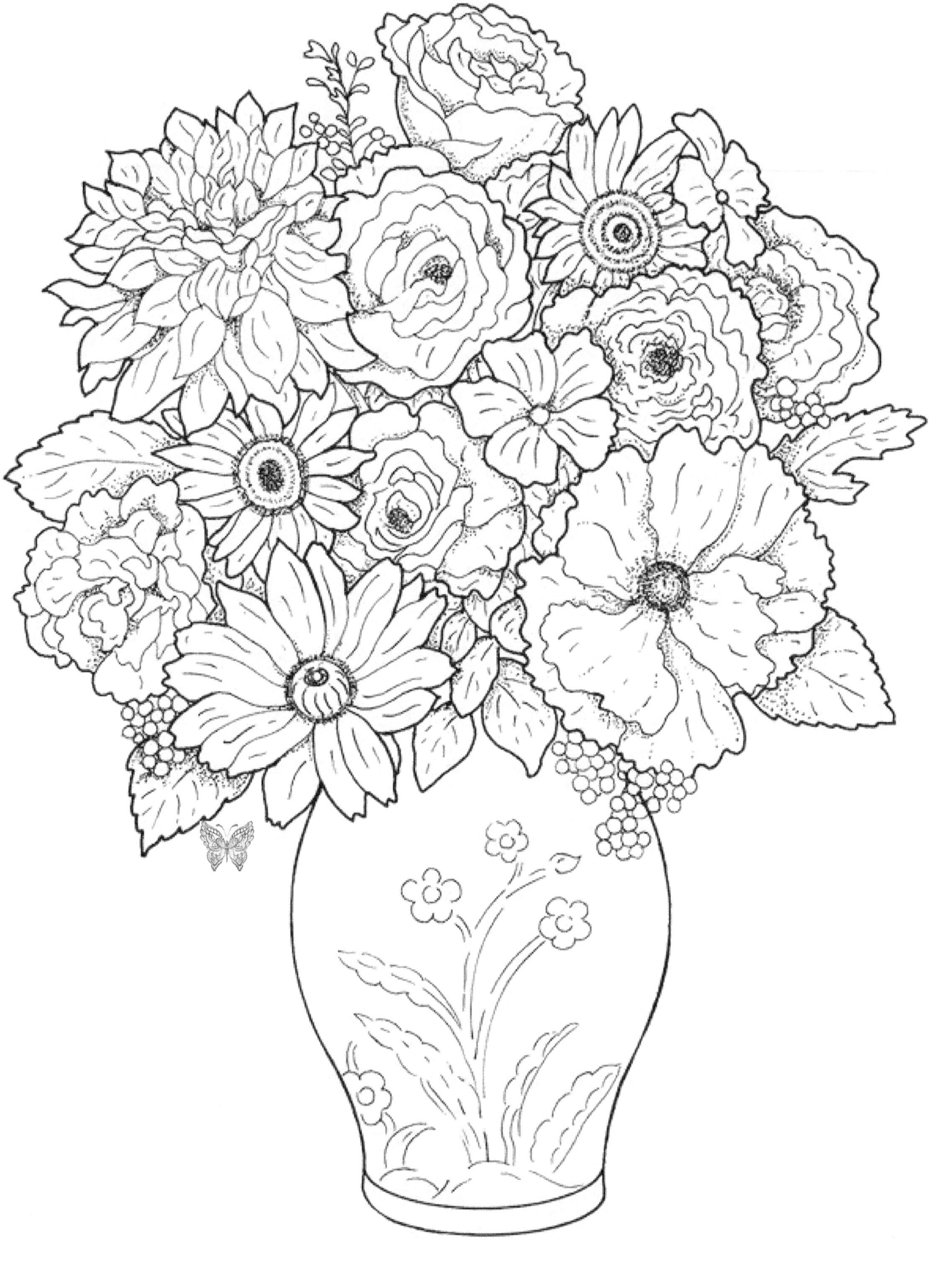

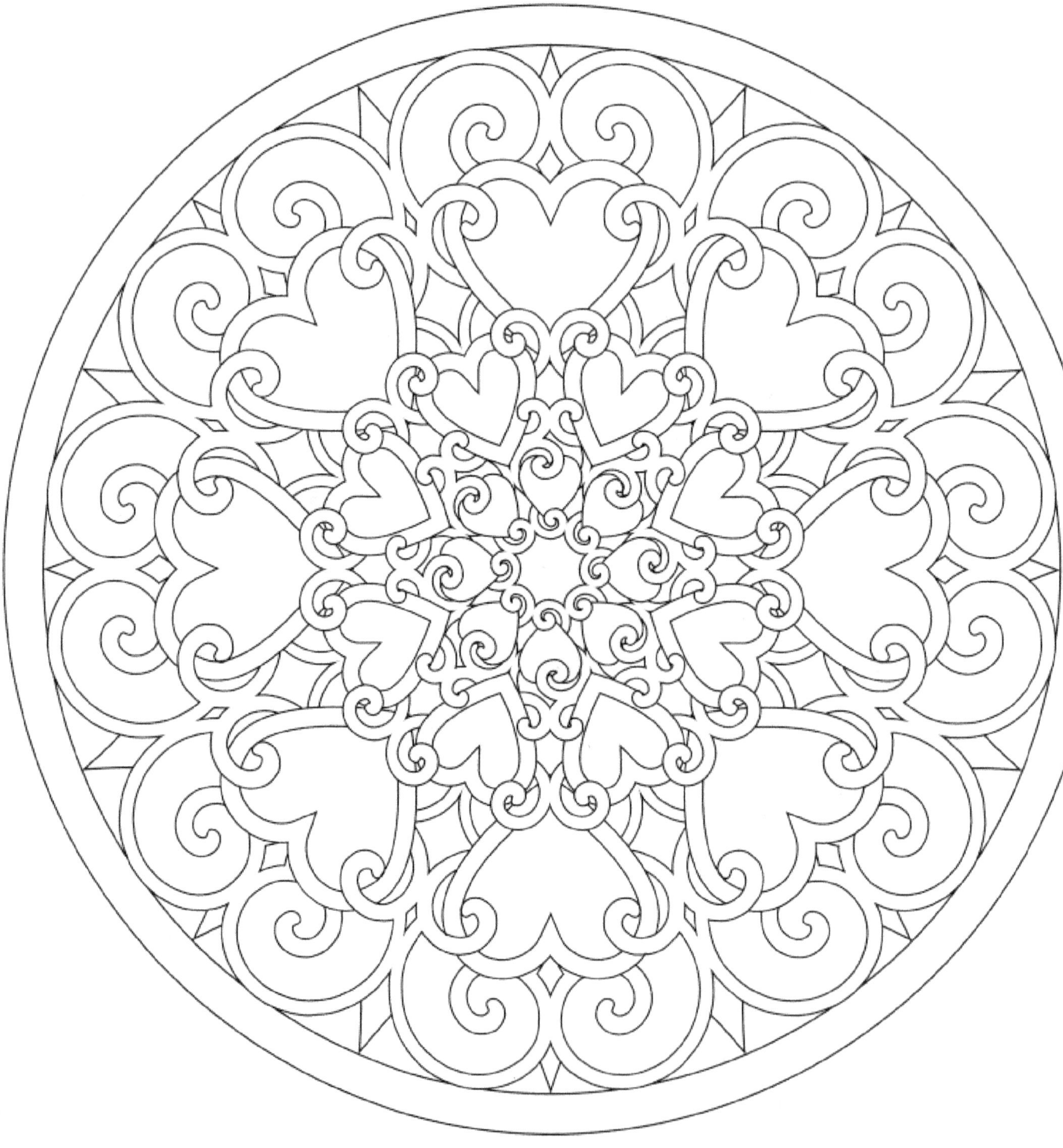

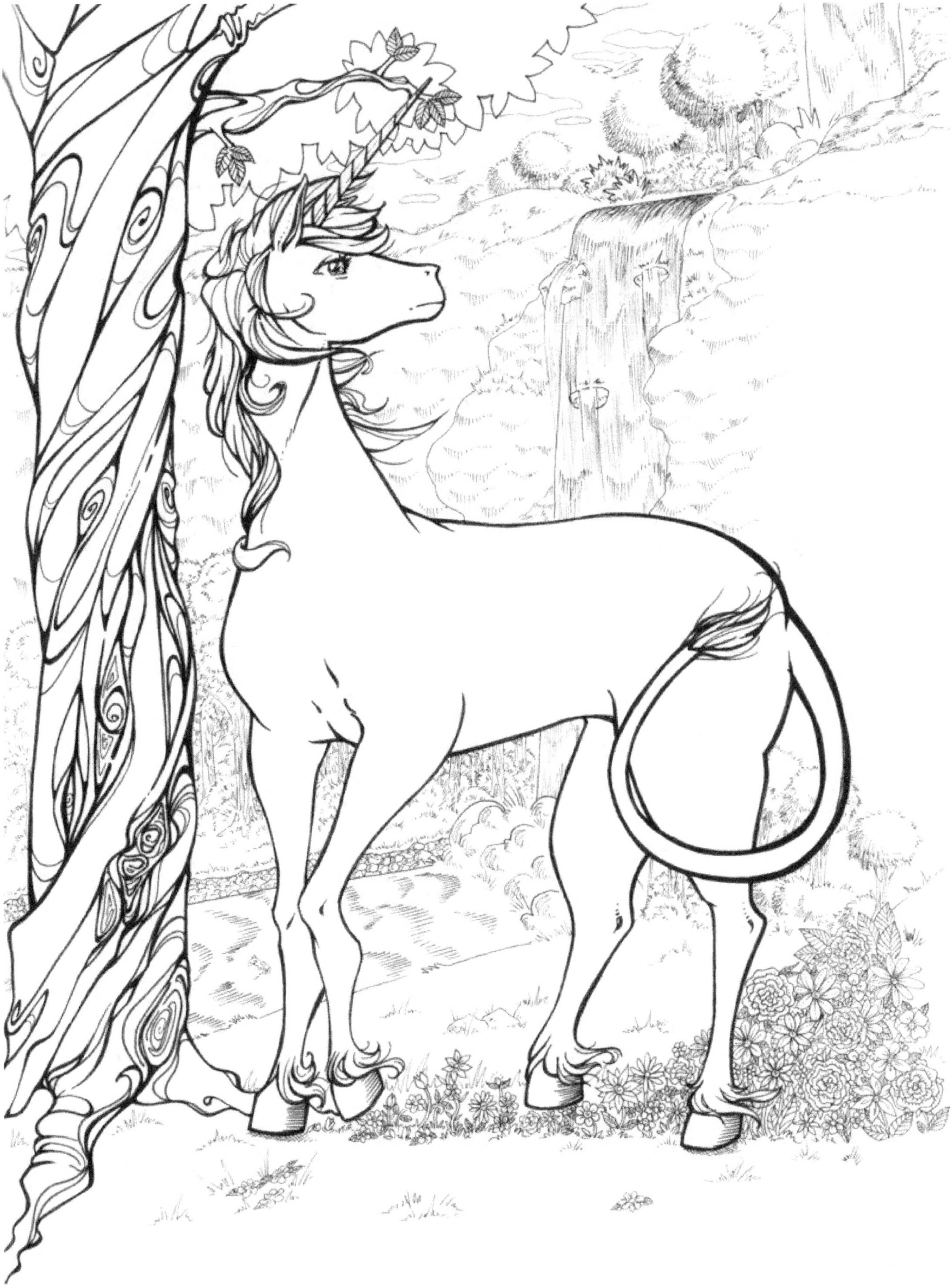

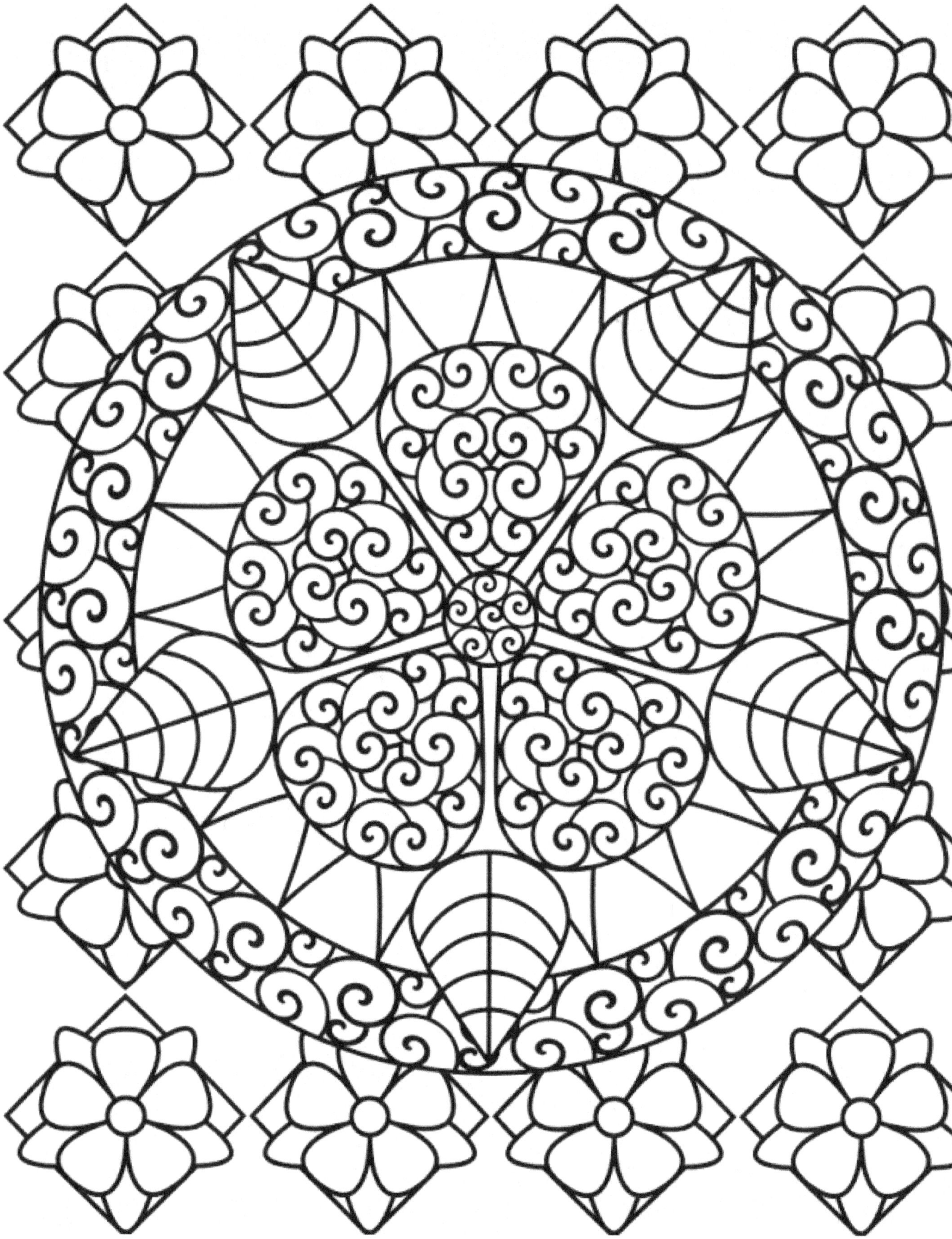

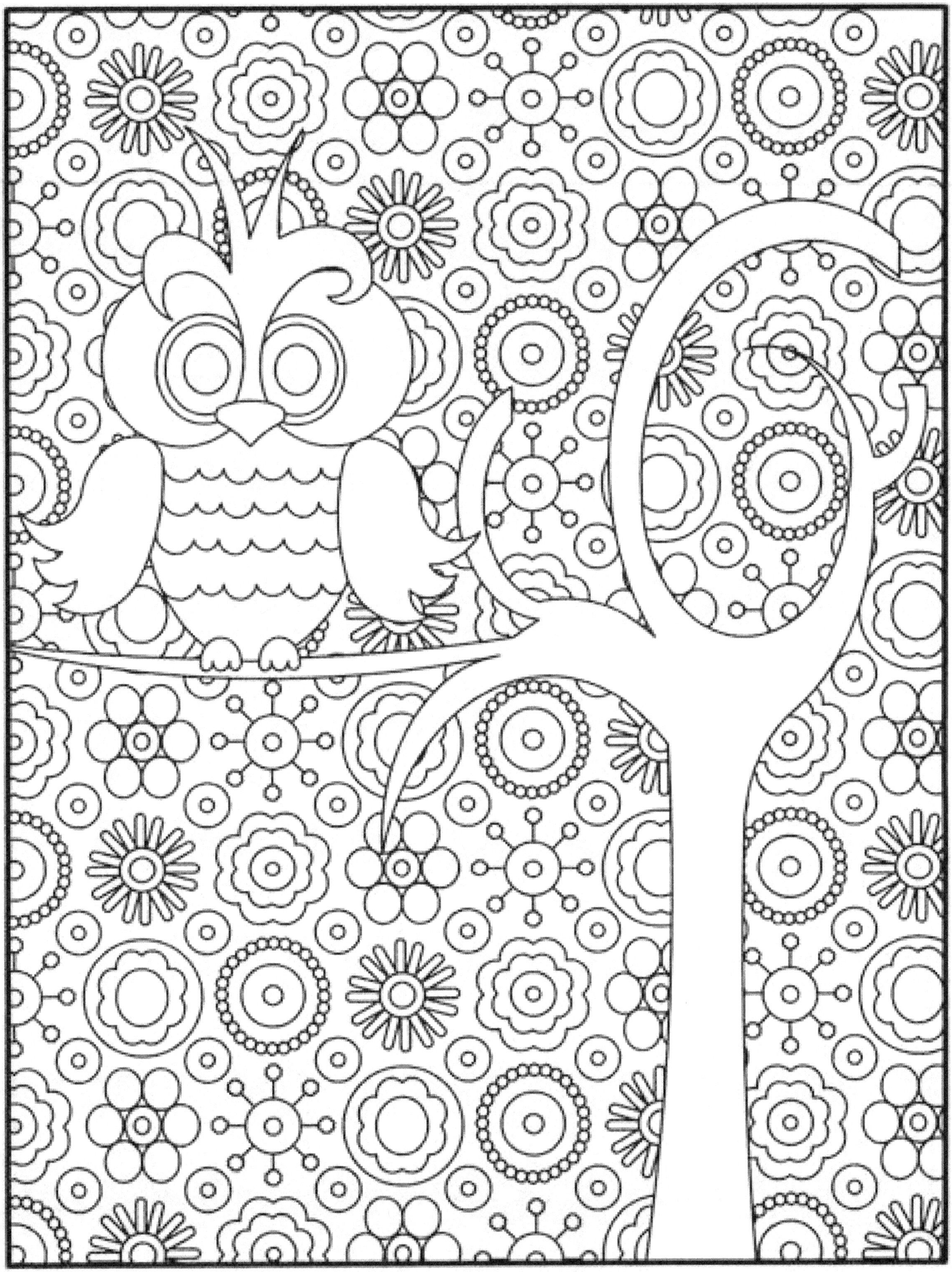

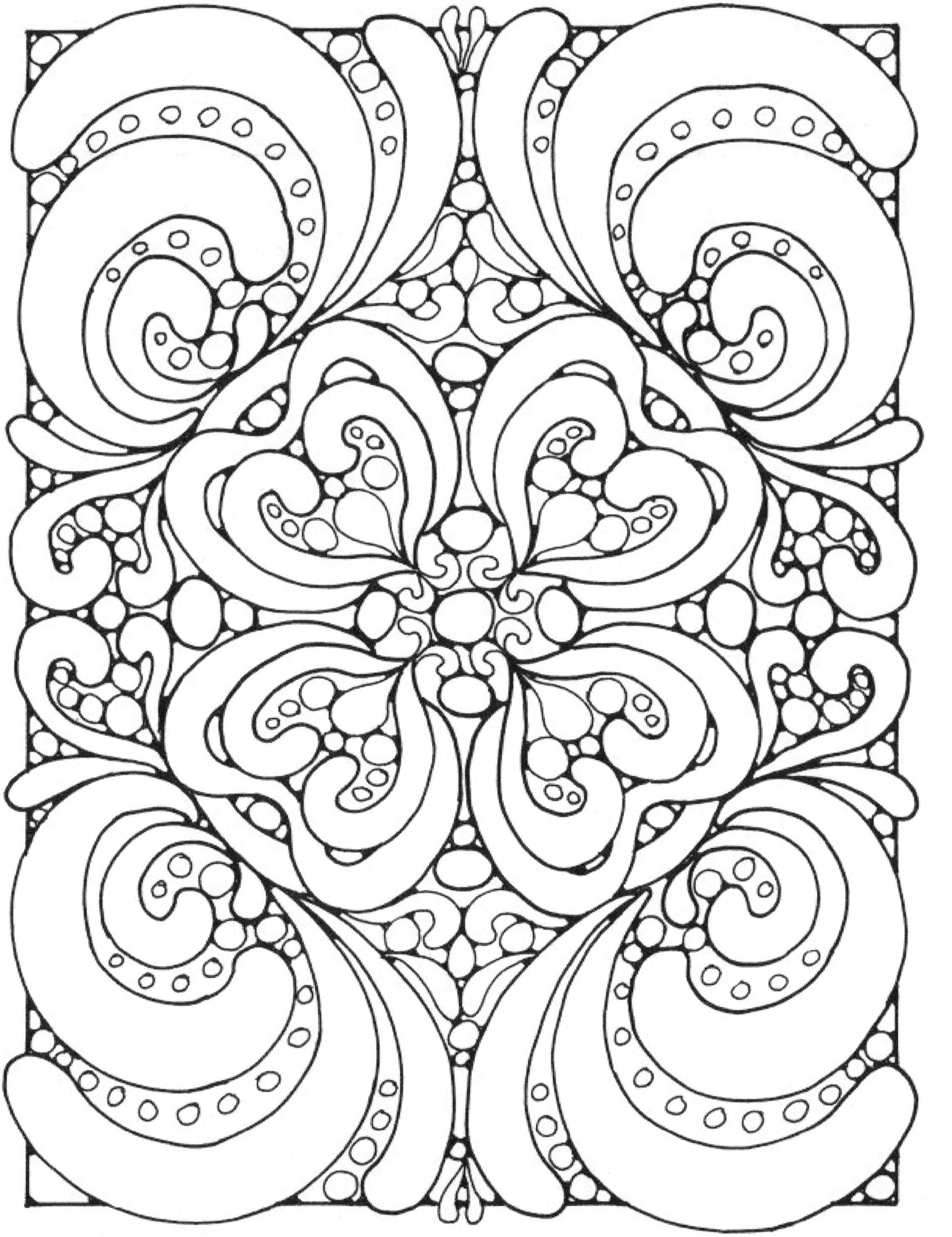

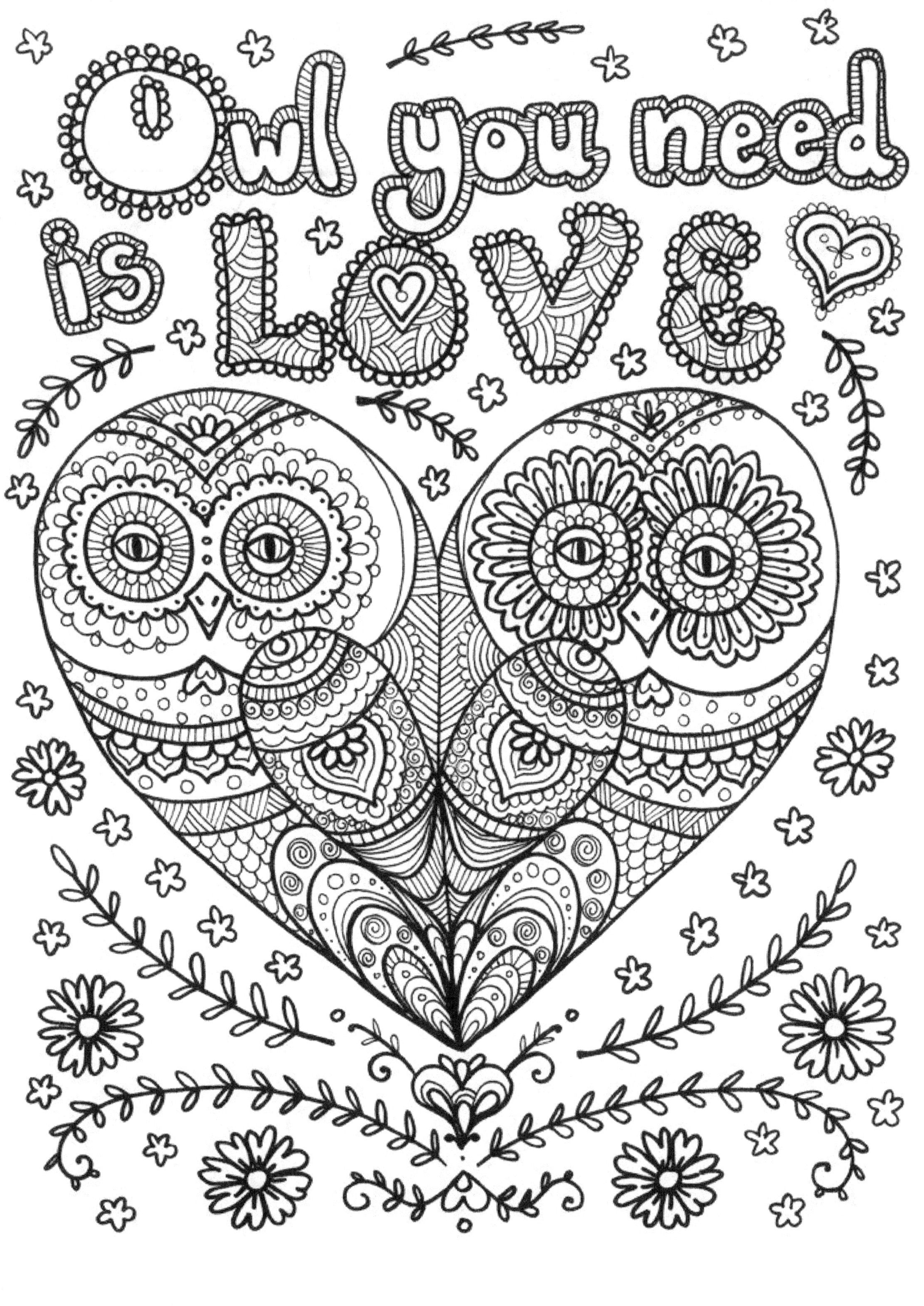
Owl you need
is LOVE

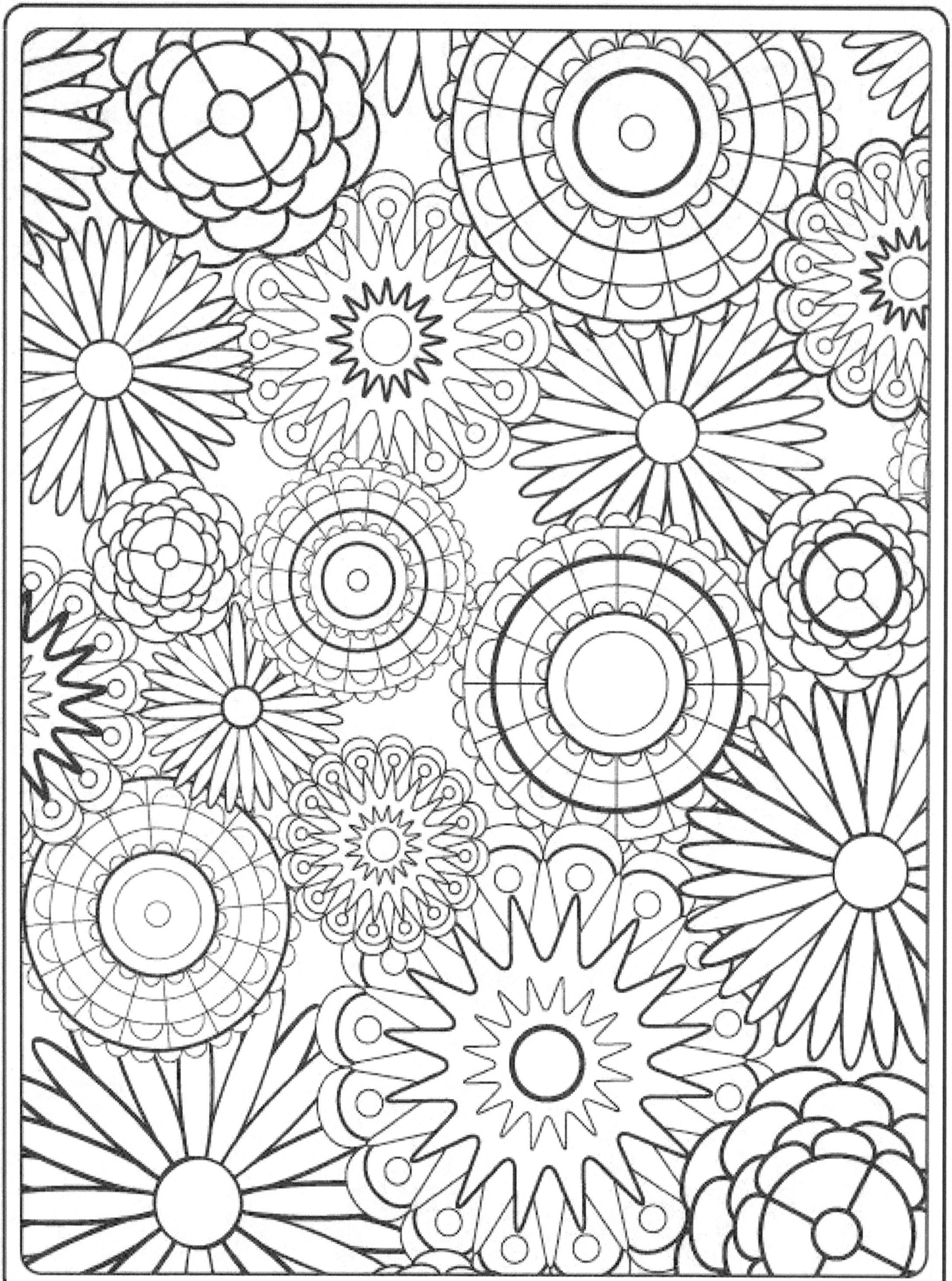

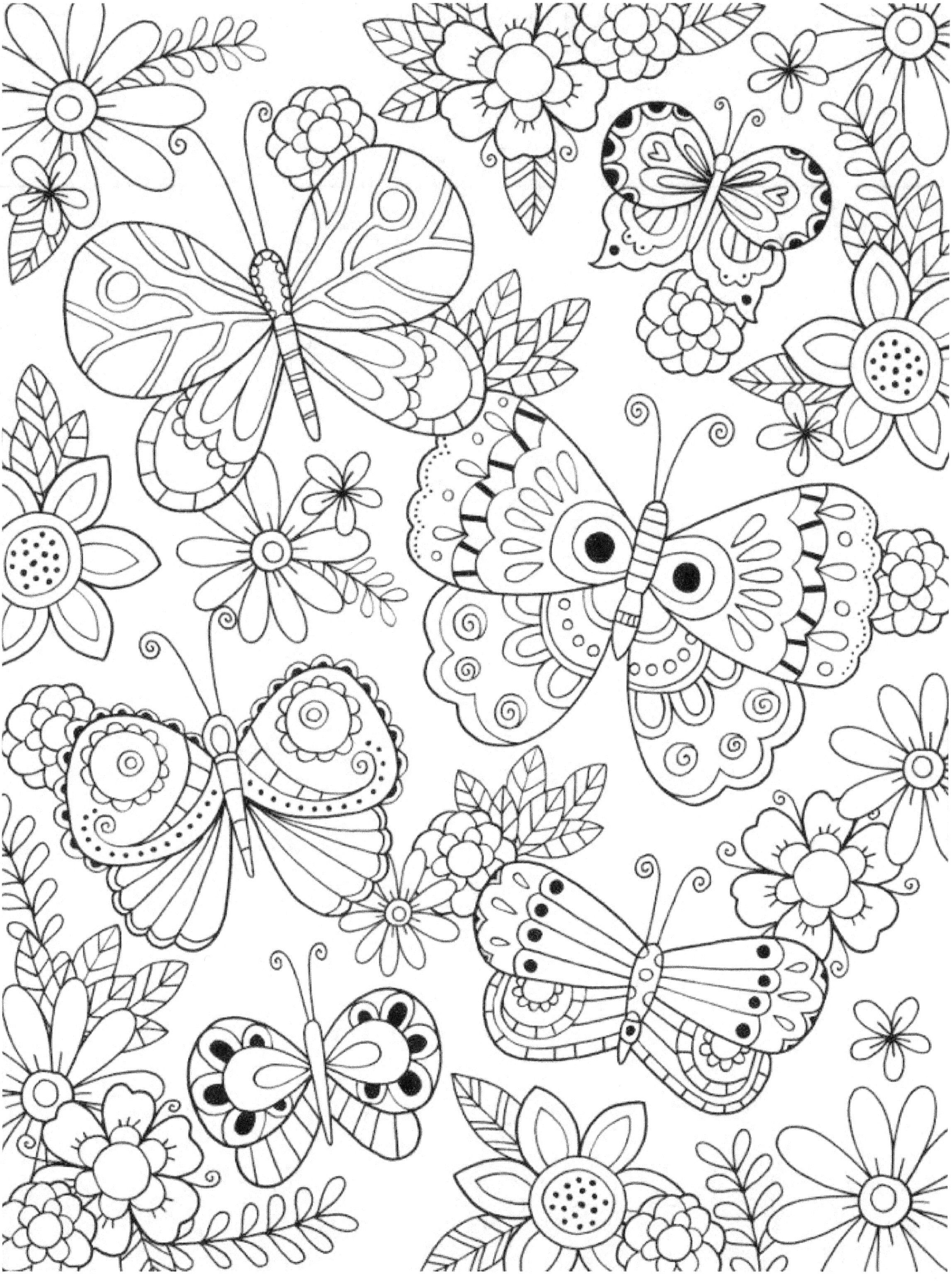

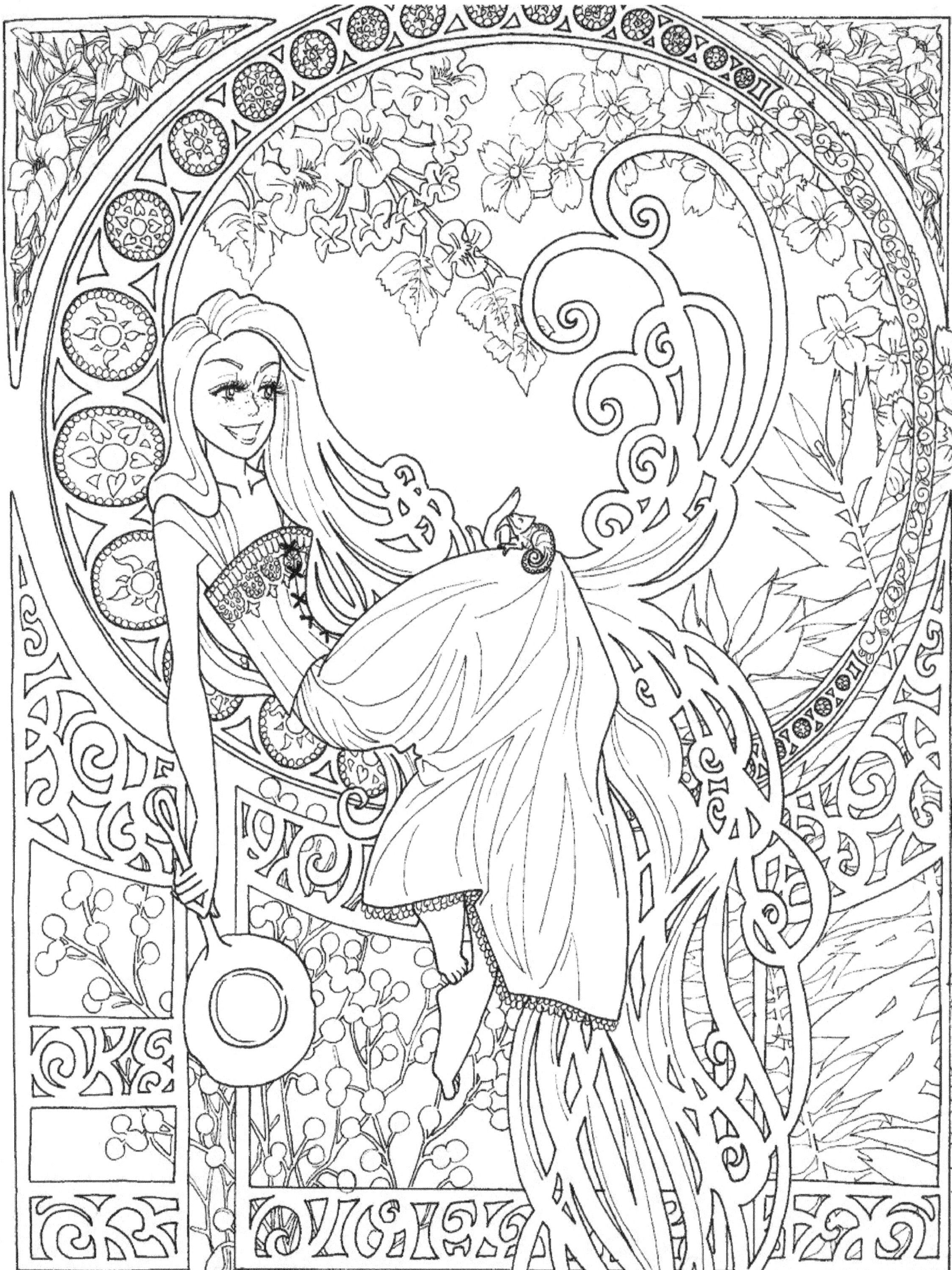

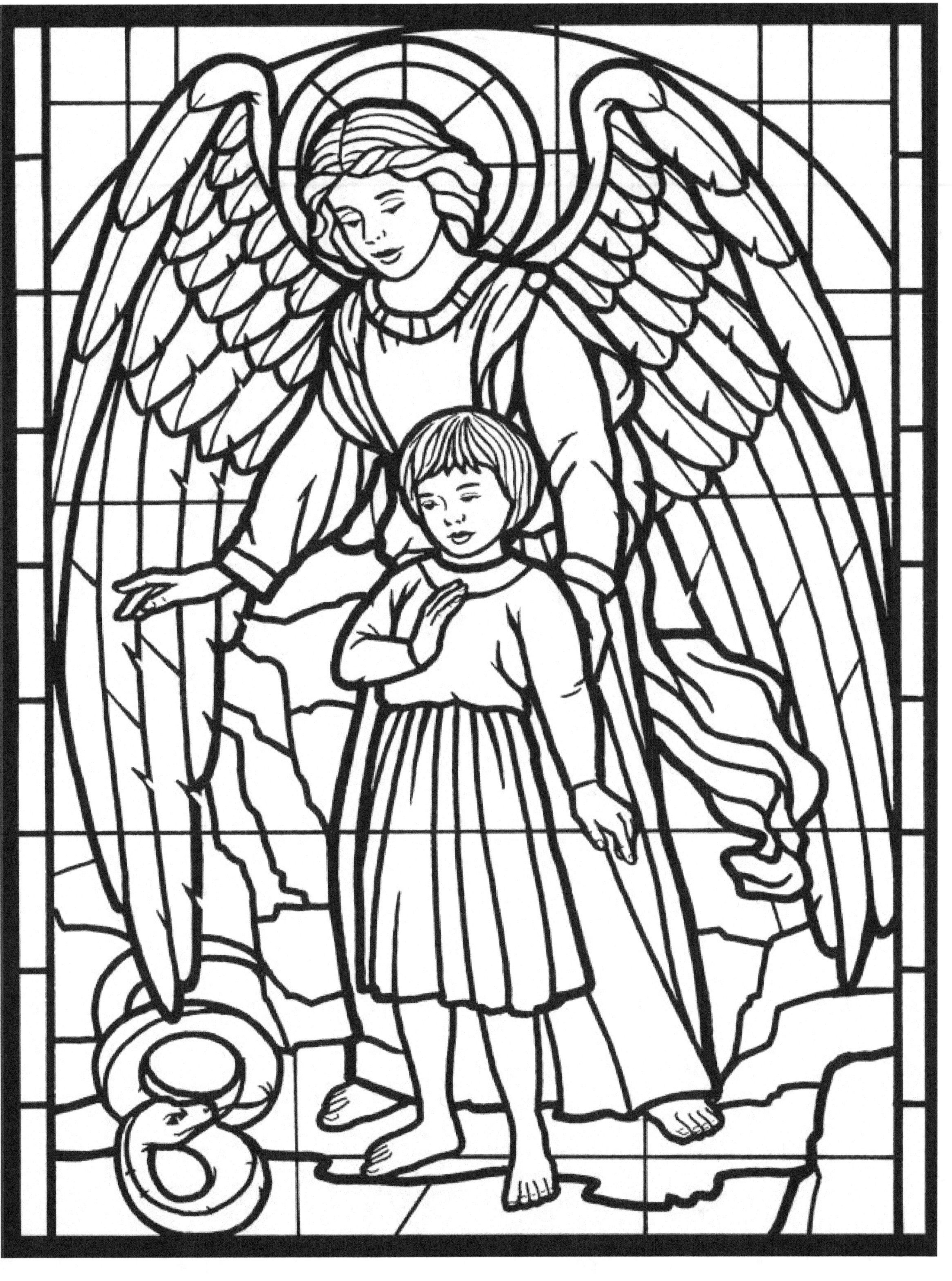

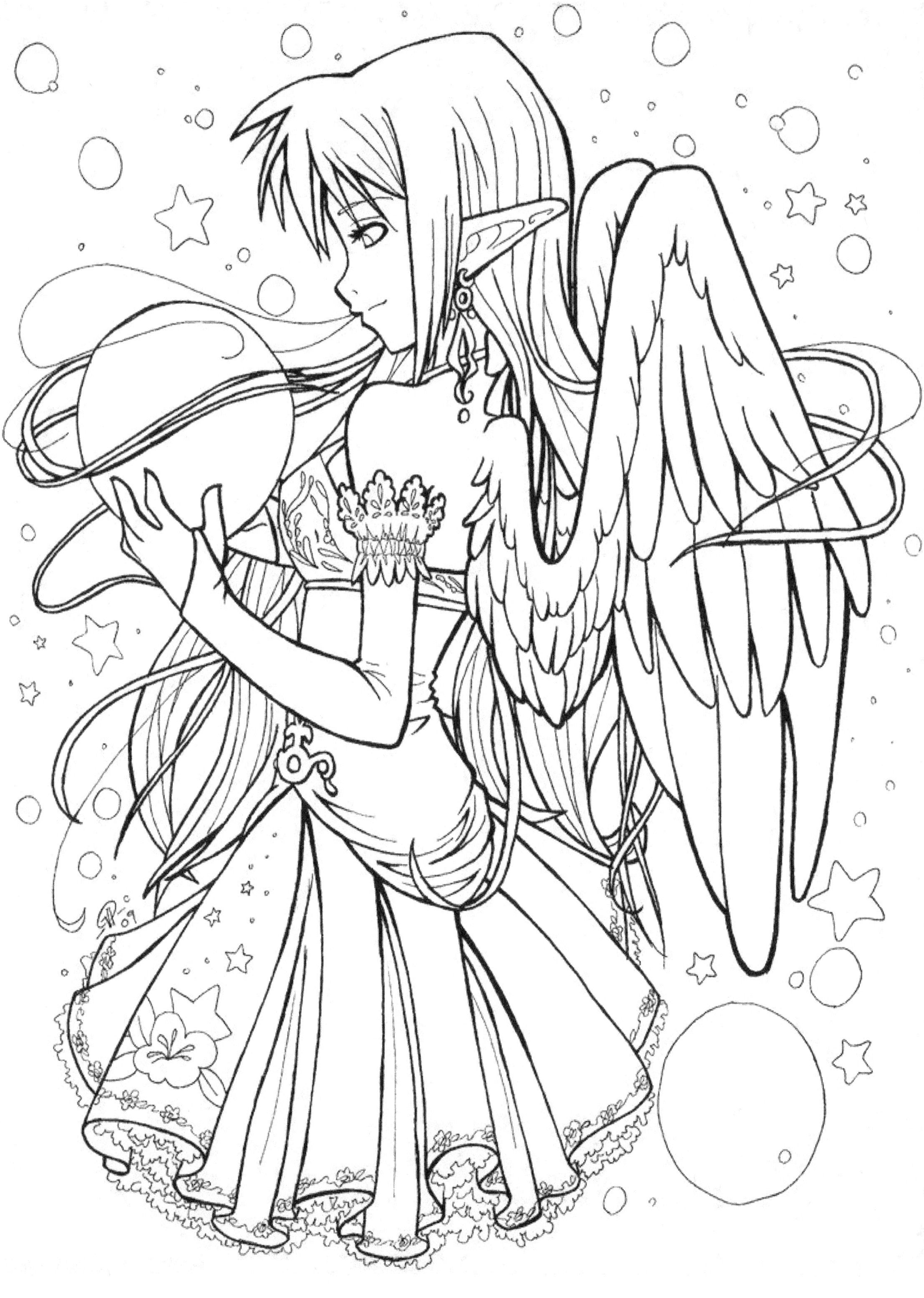

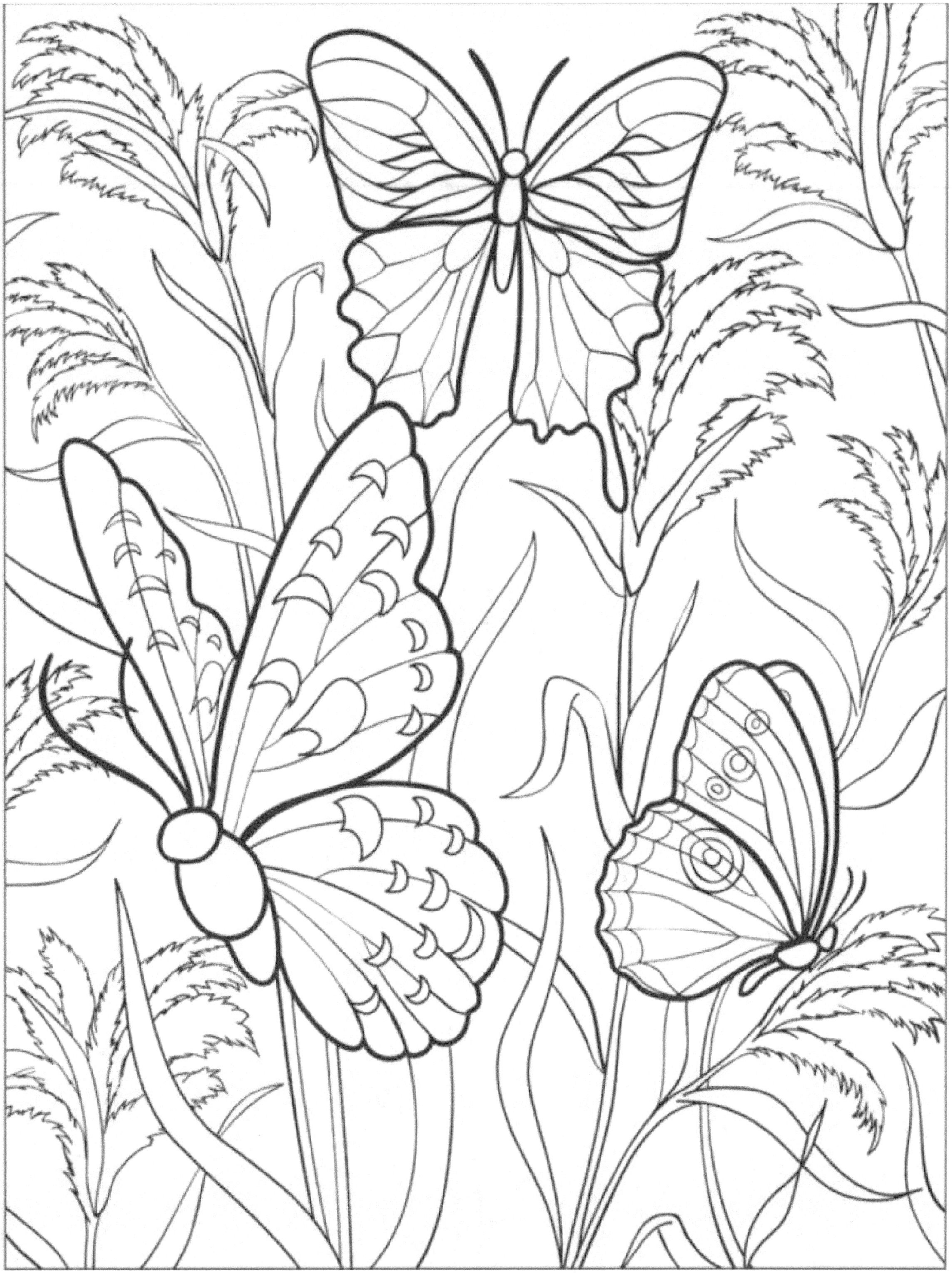

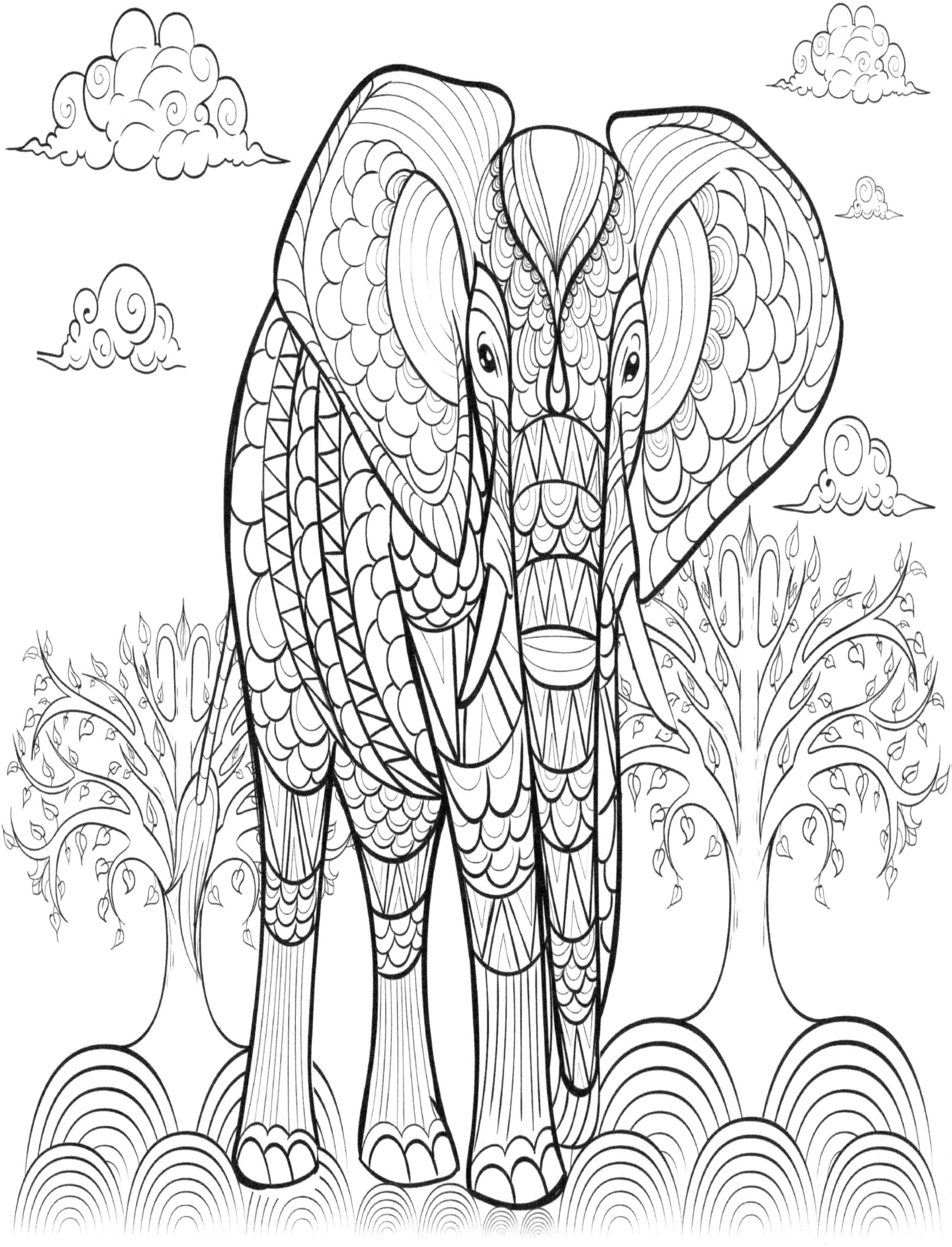

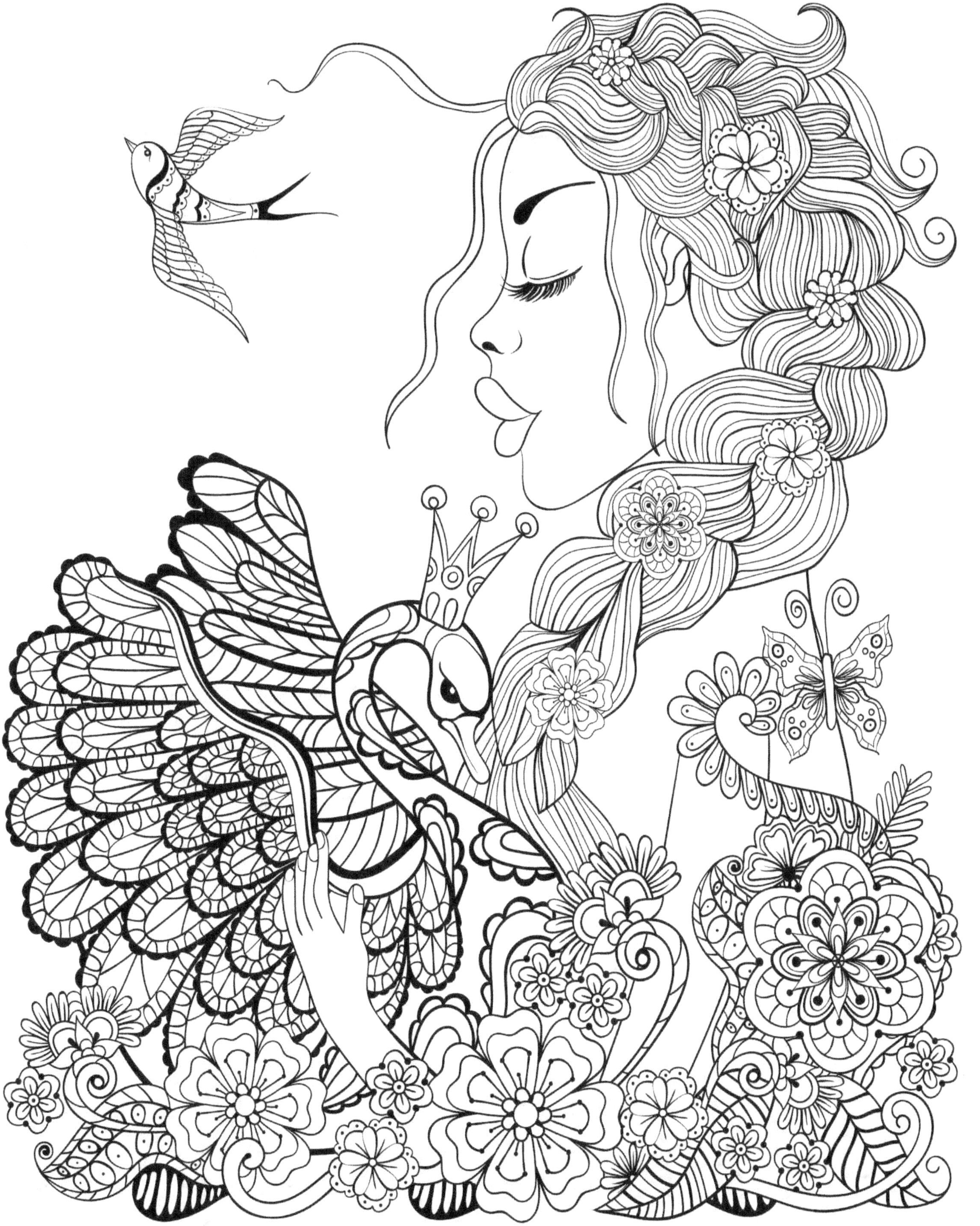

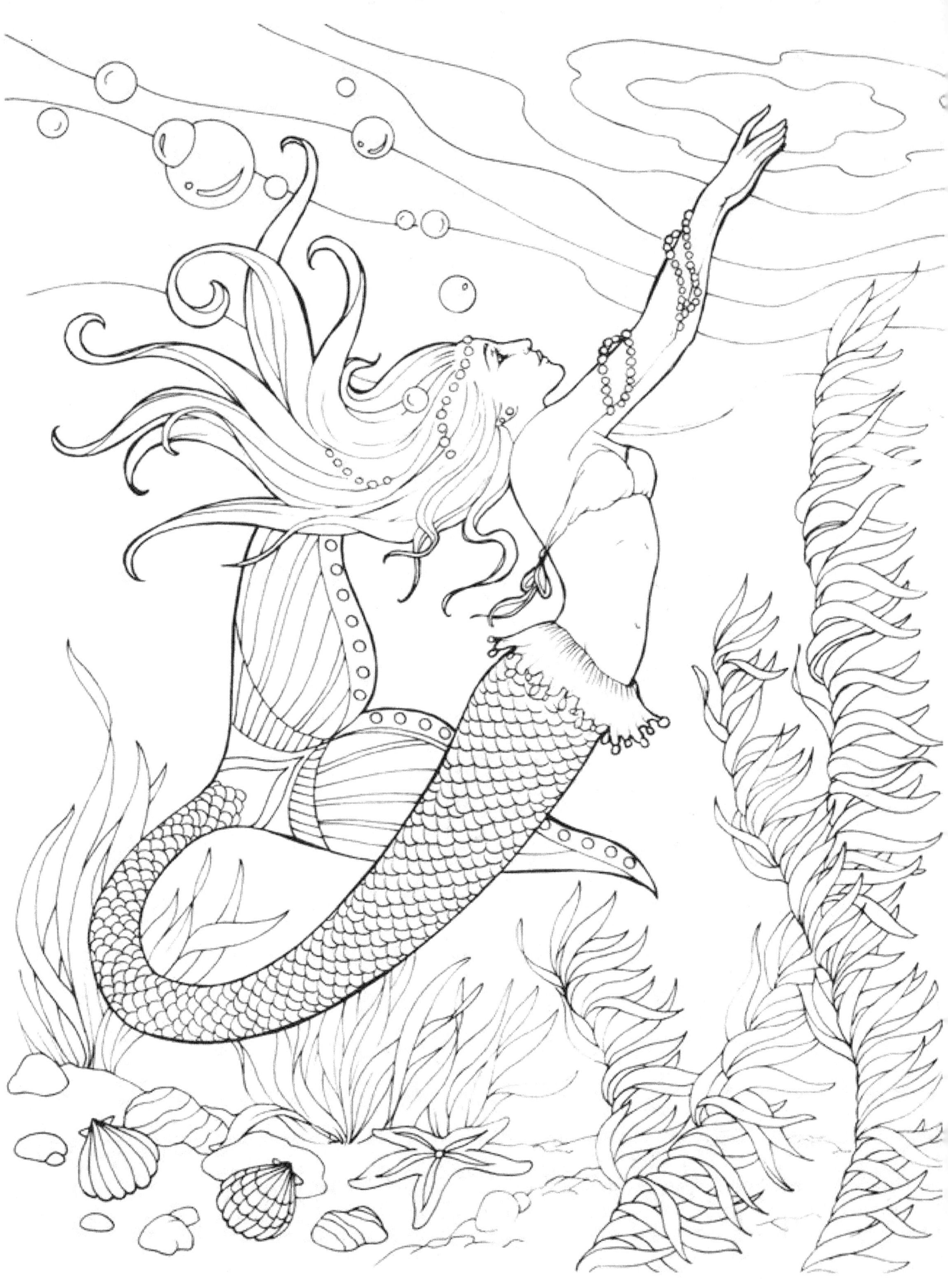

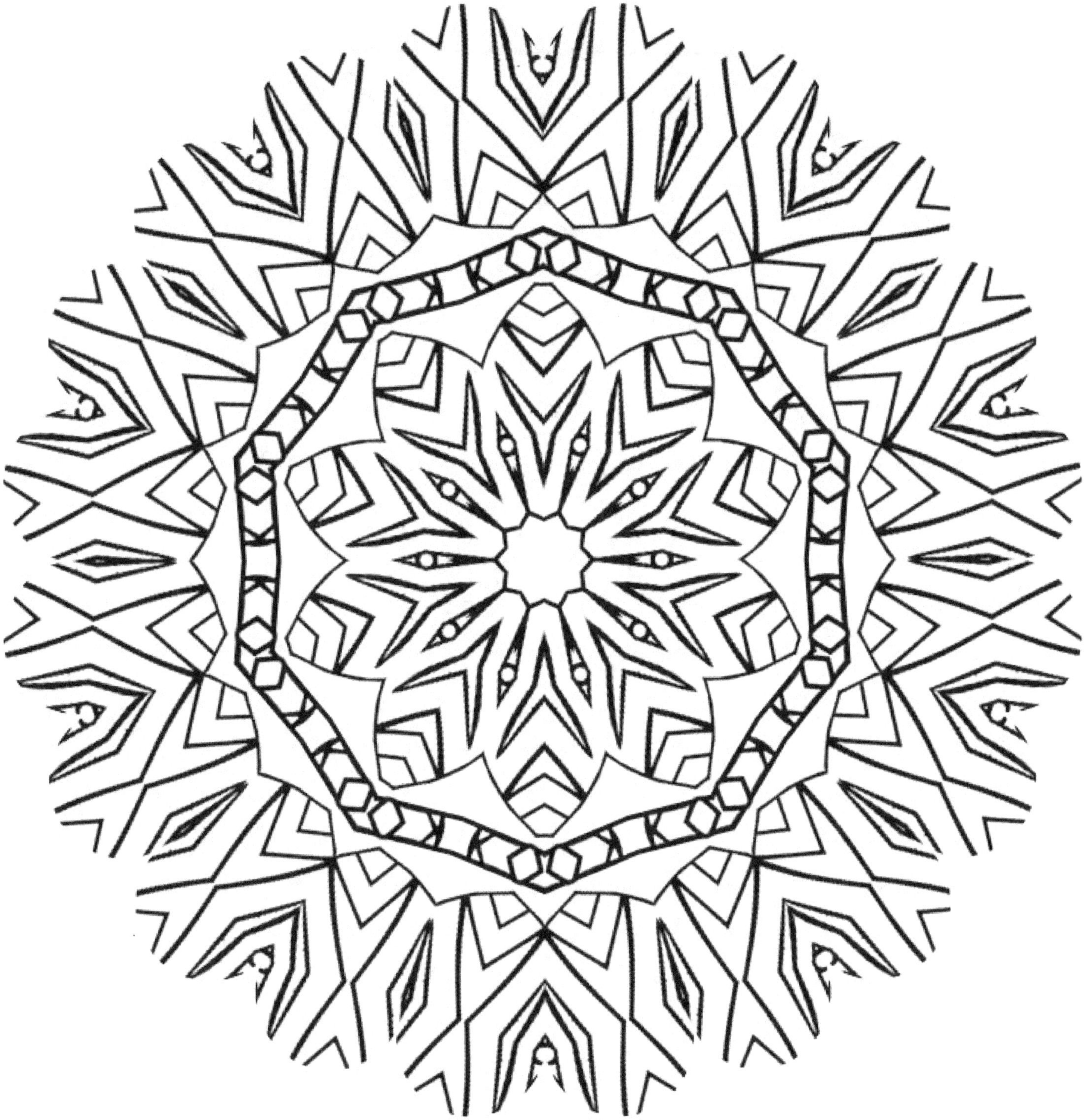

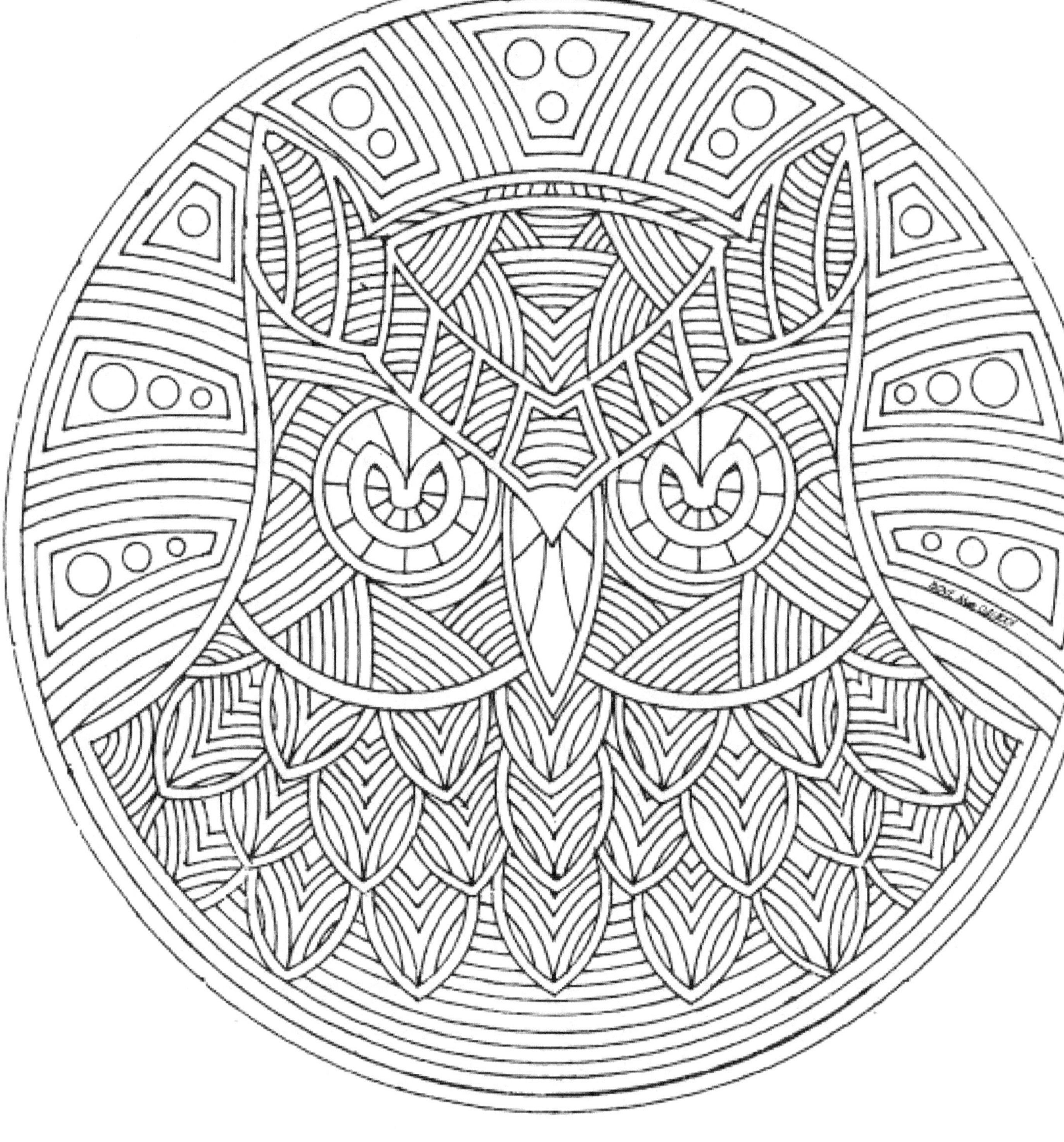

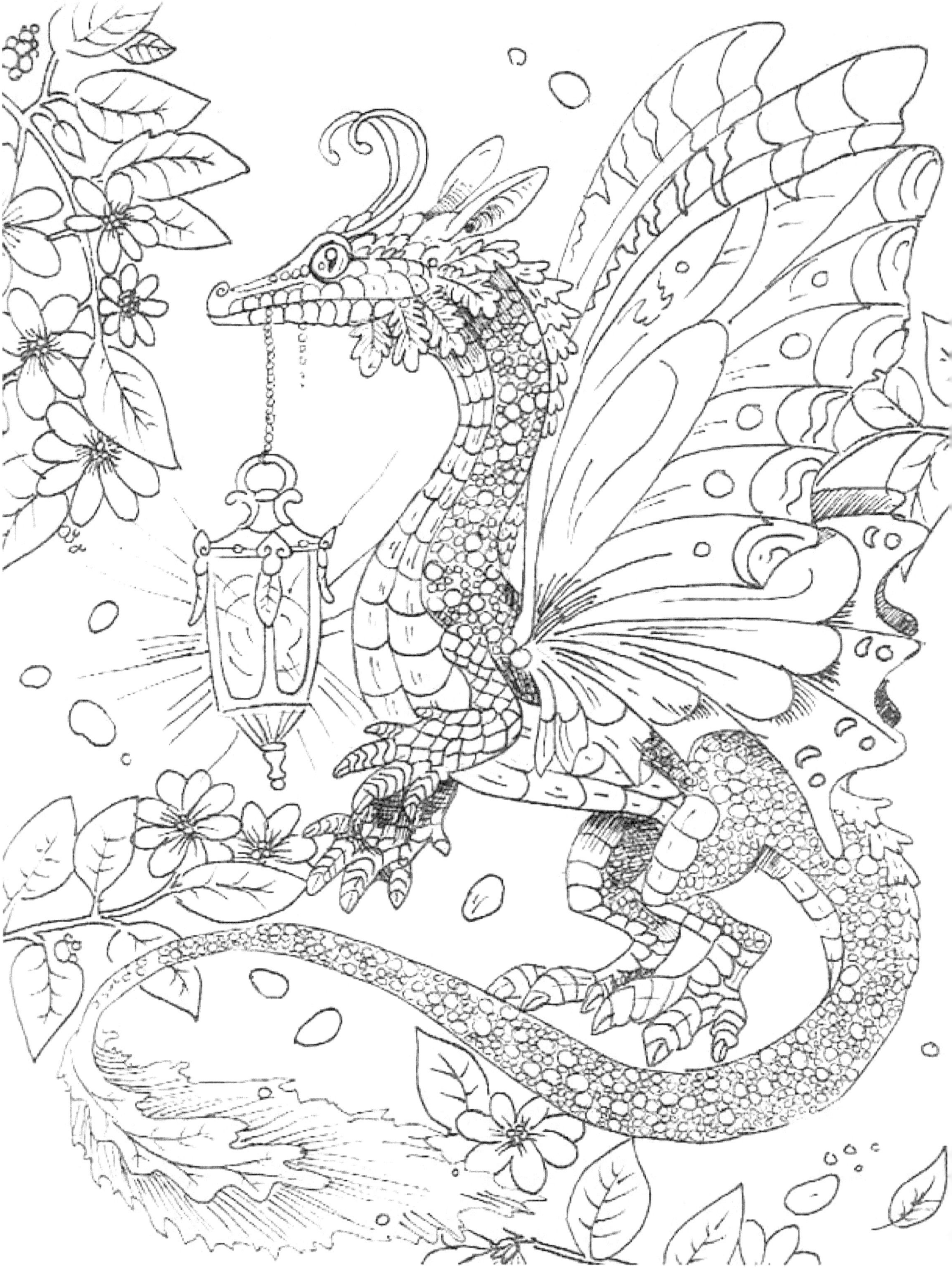

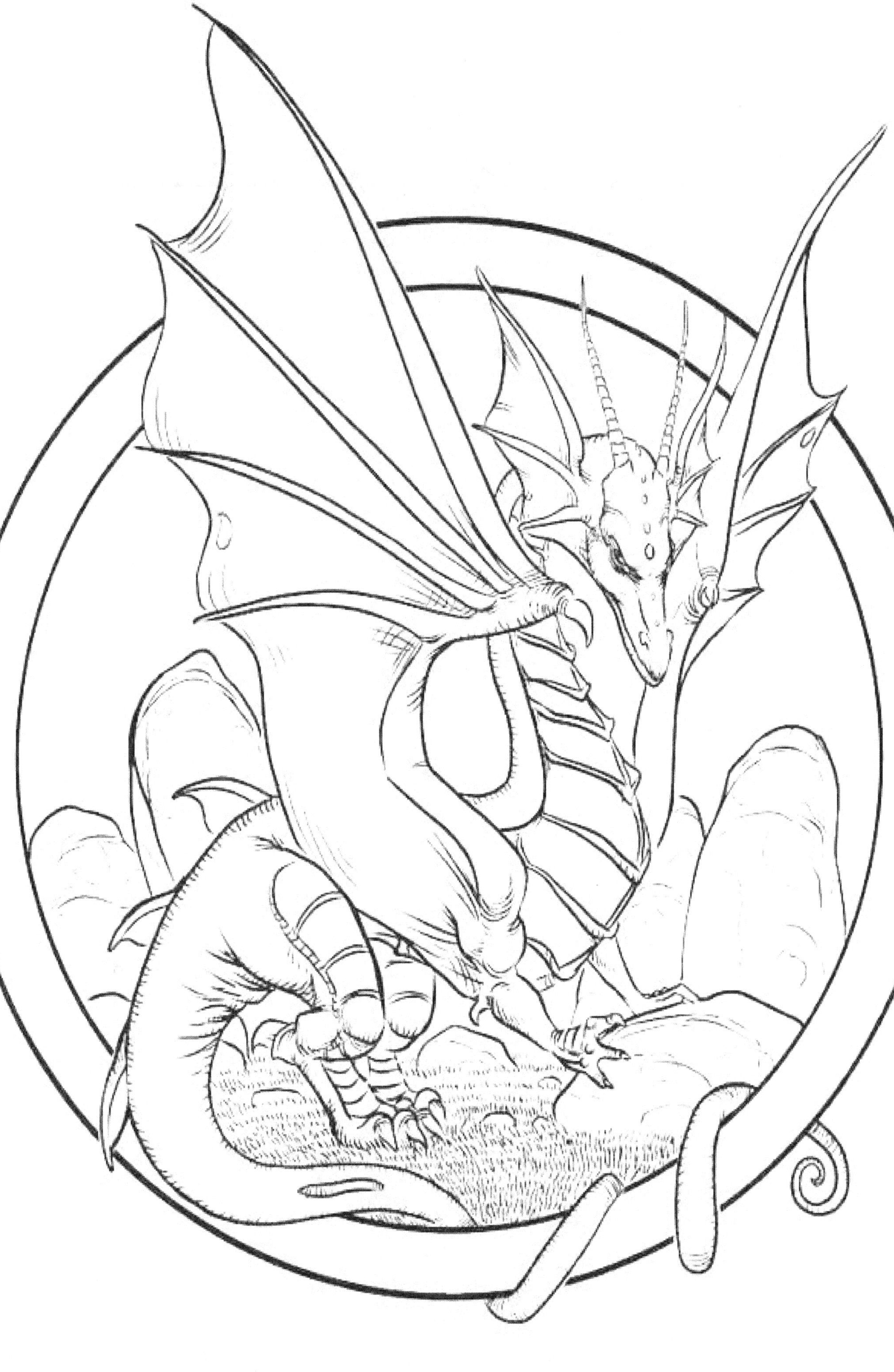

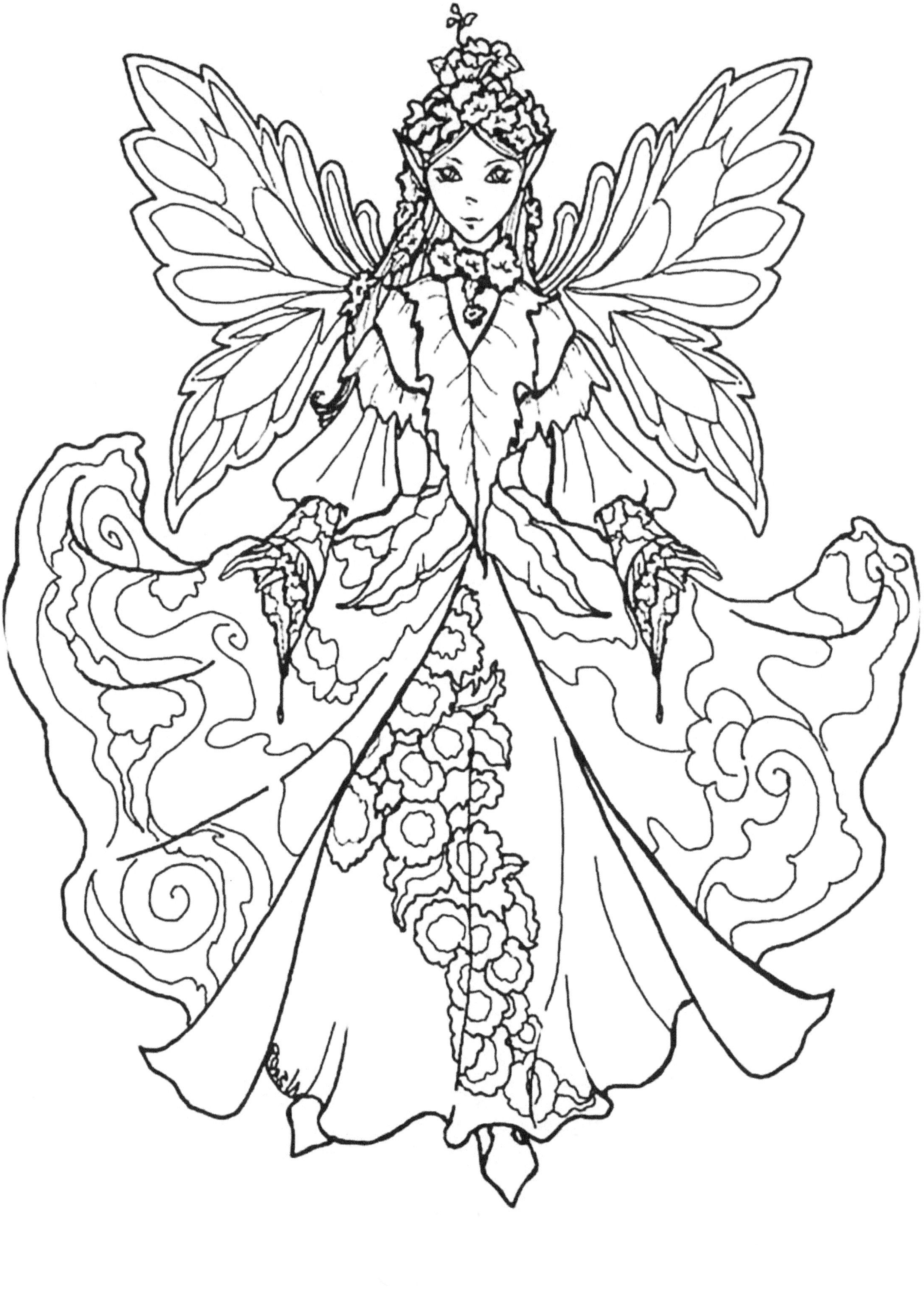

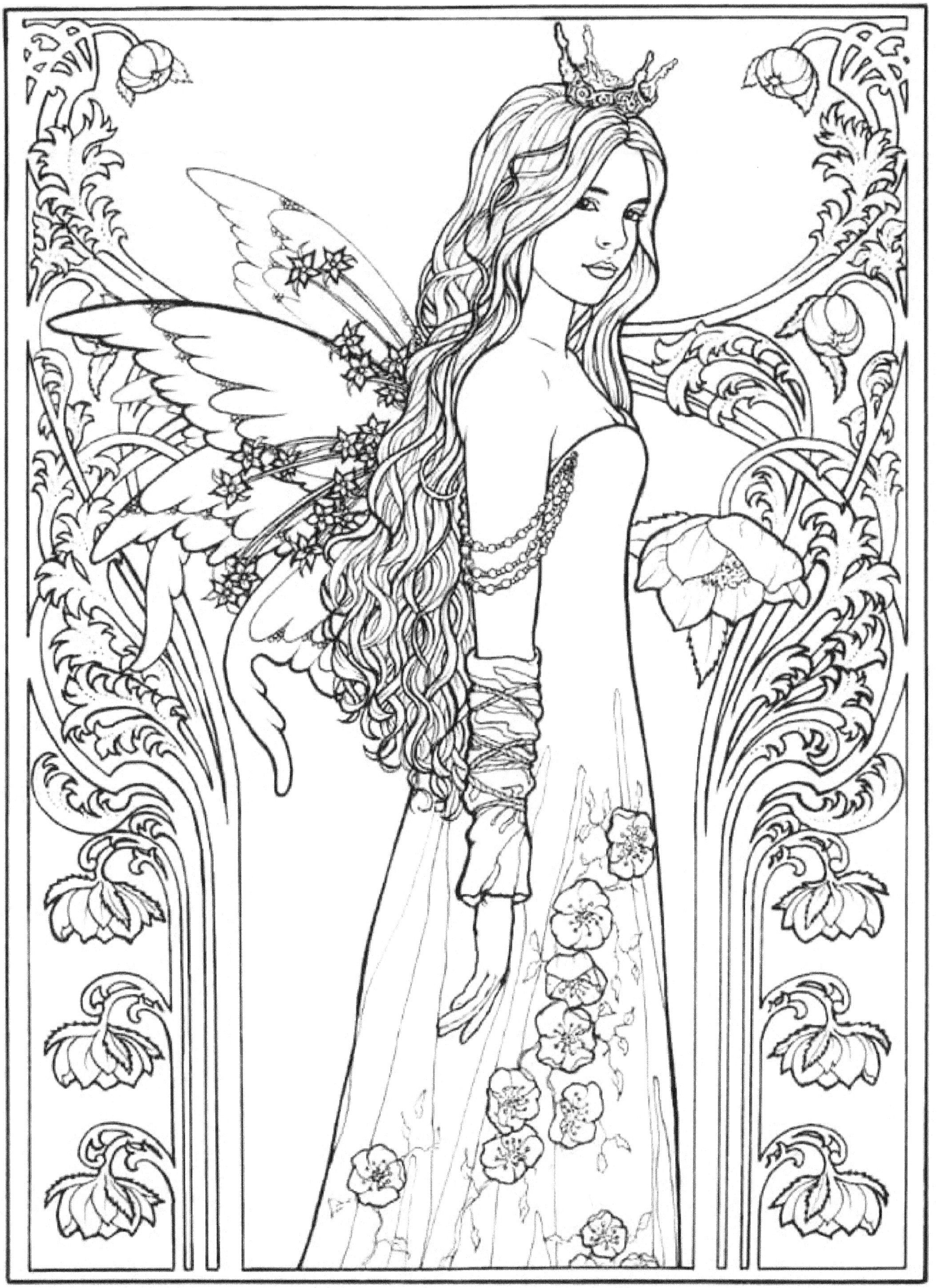

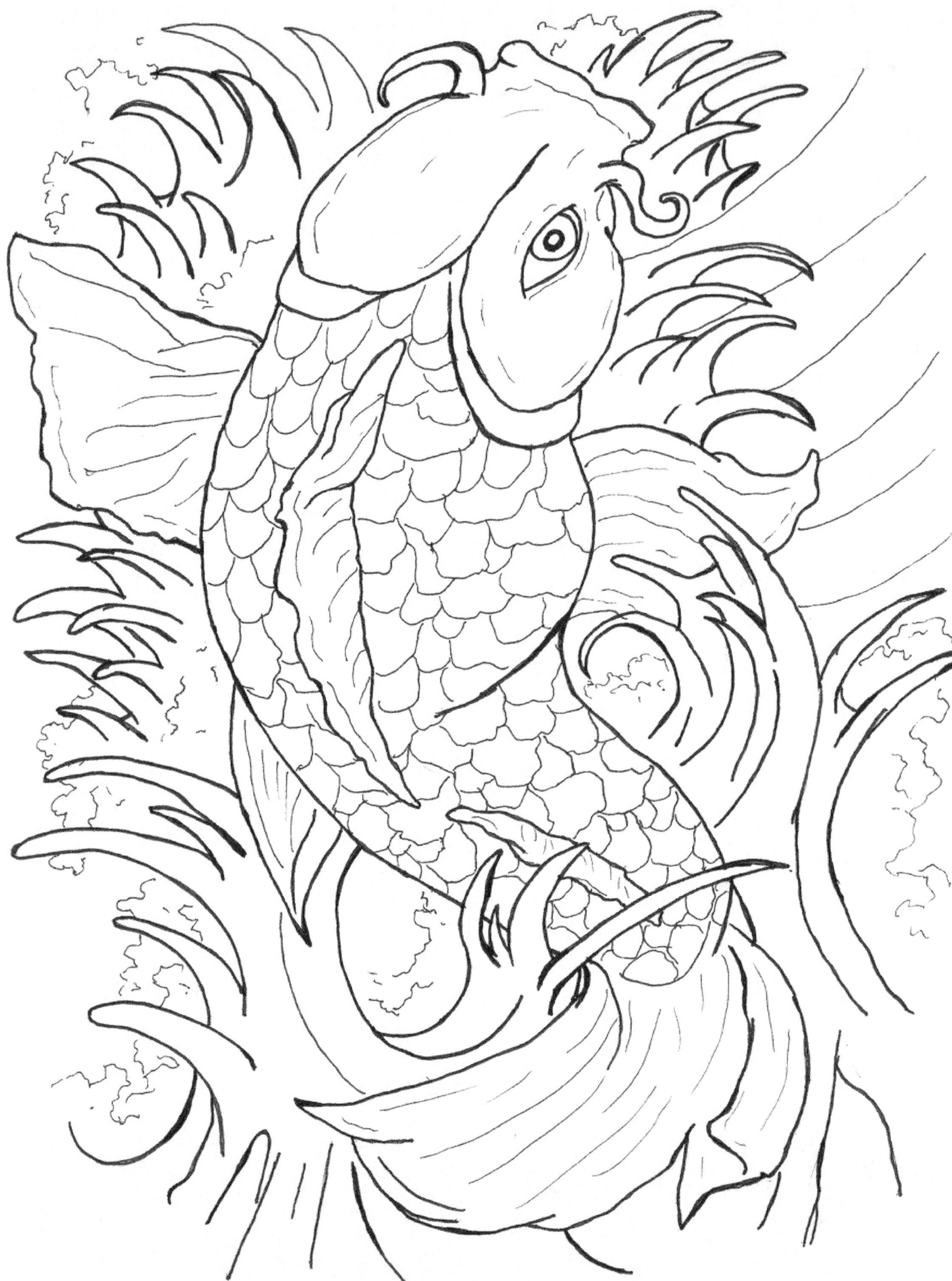

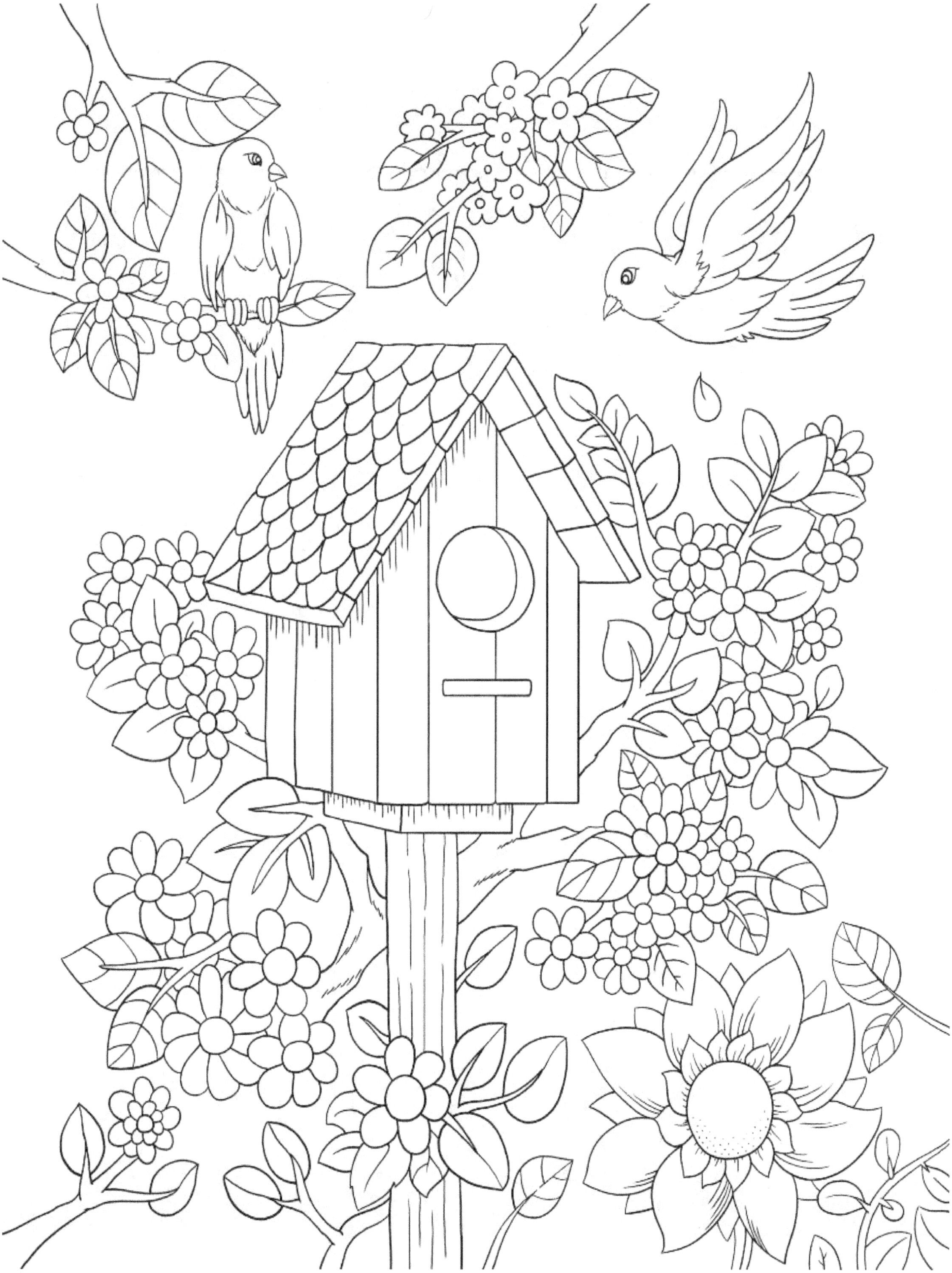

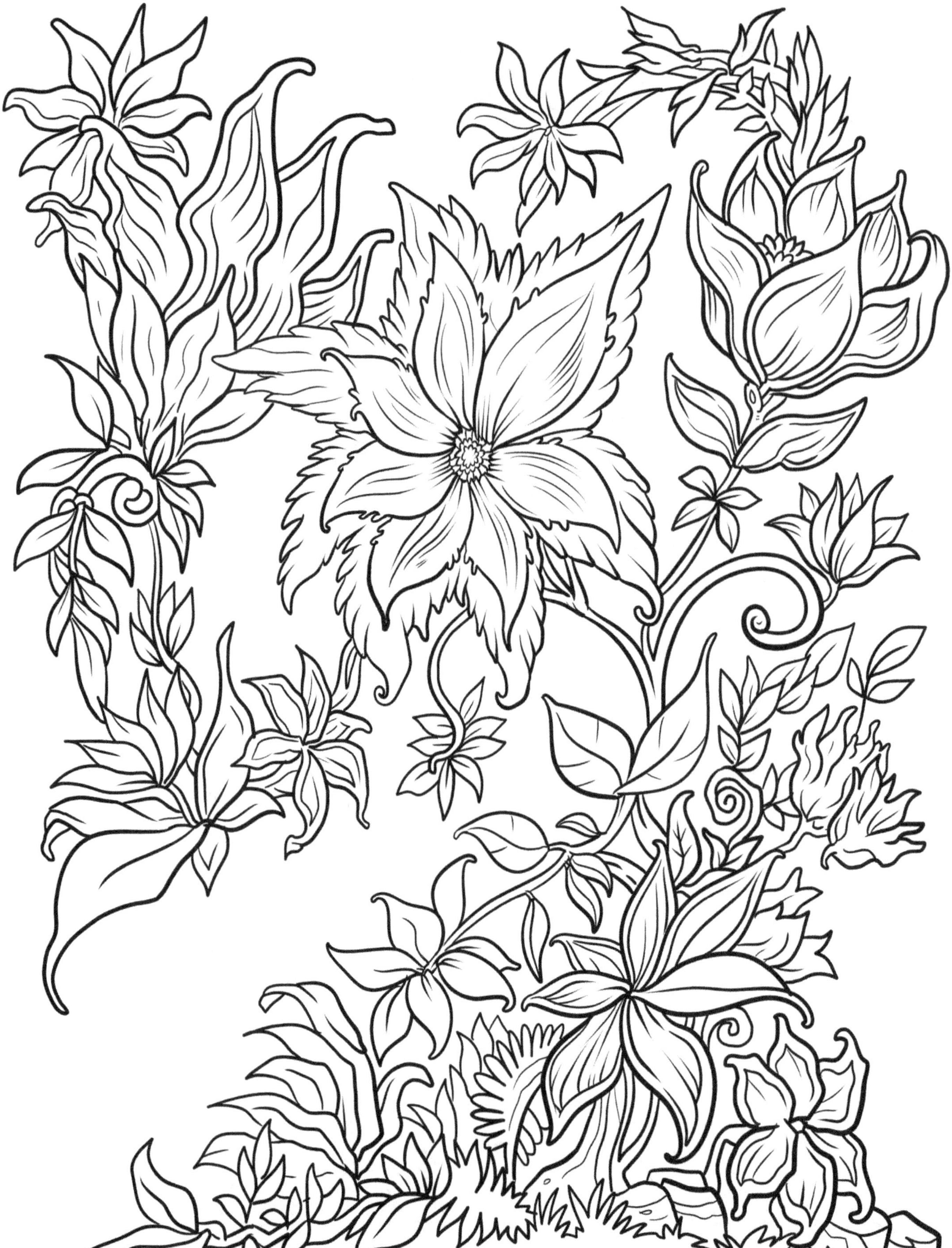

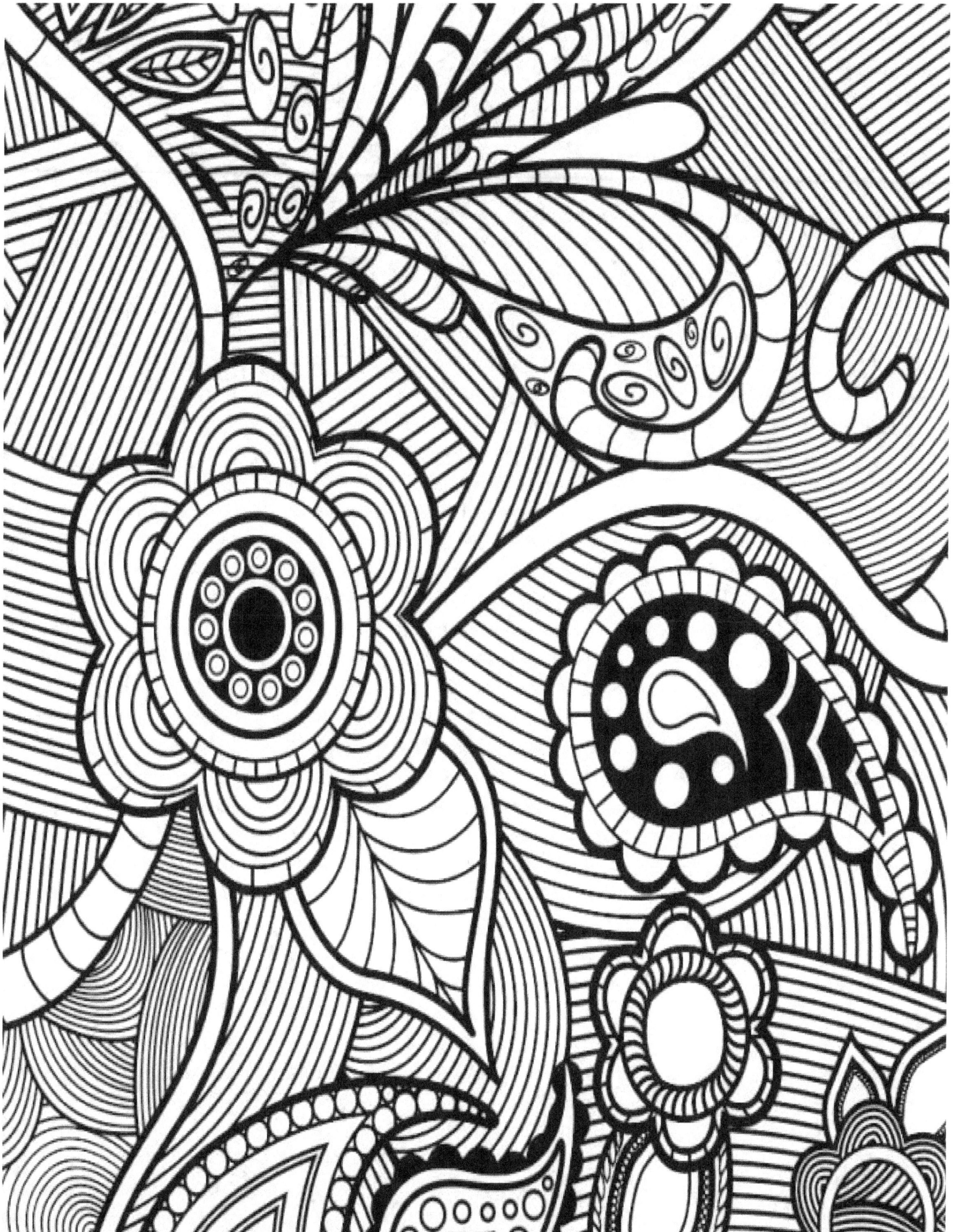

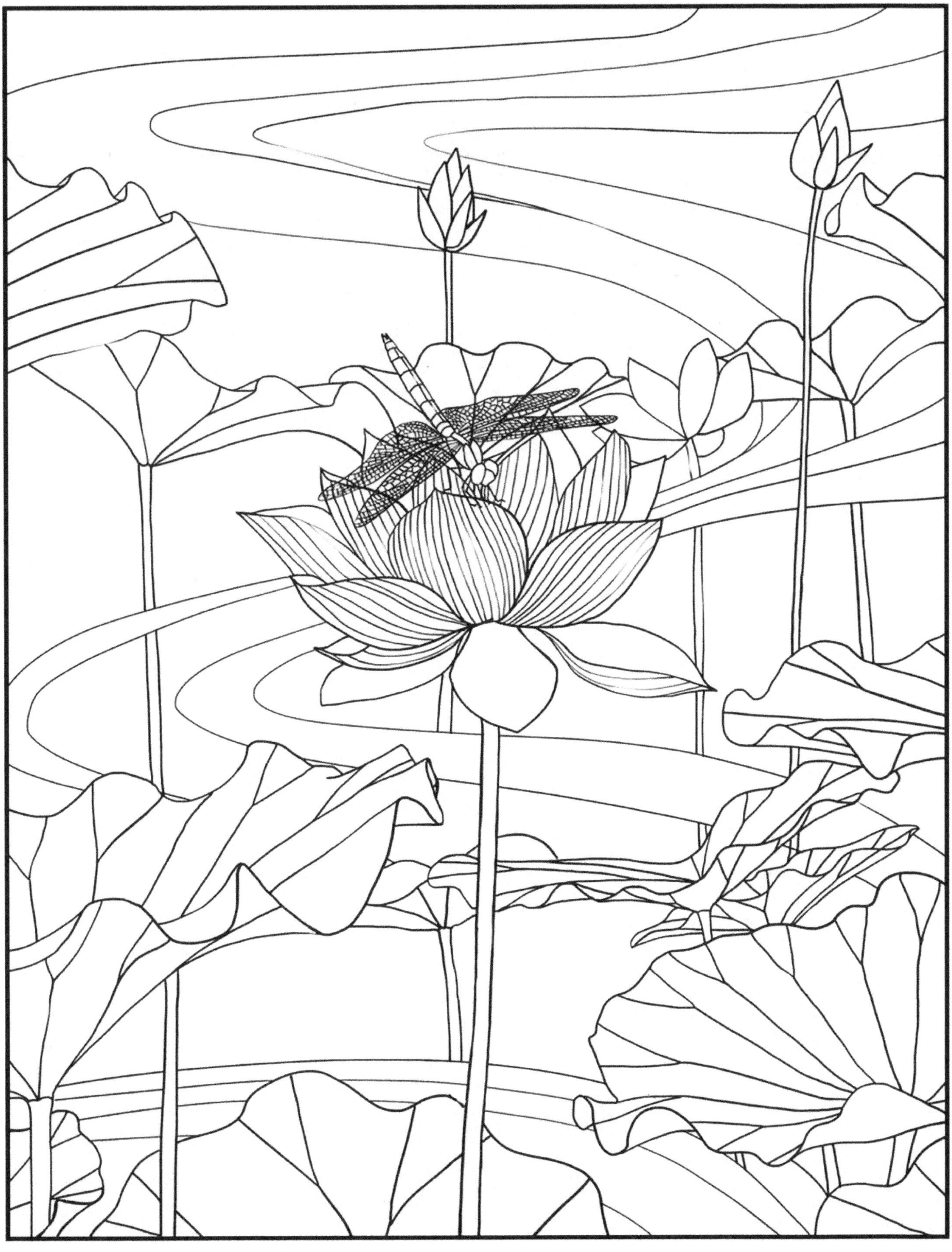

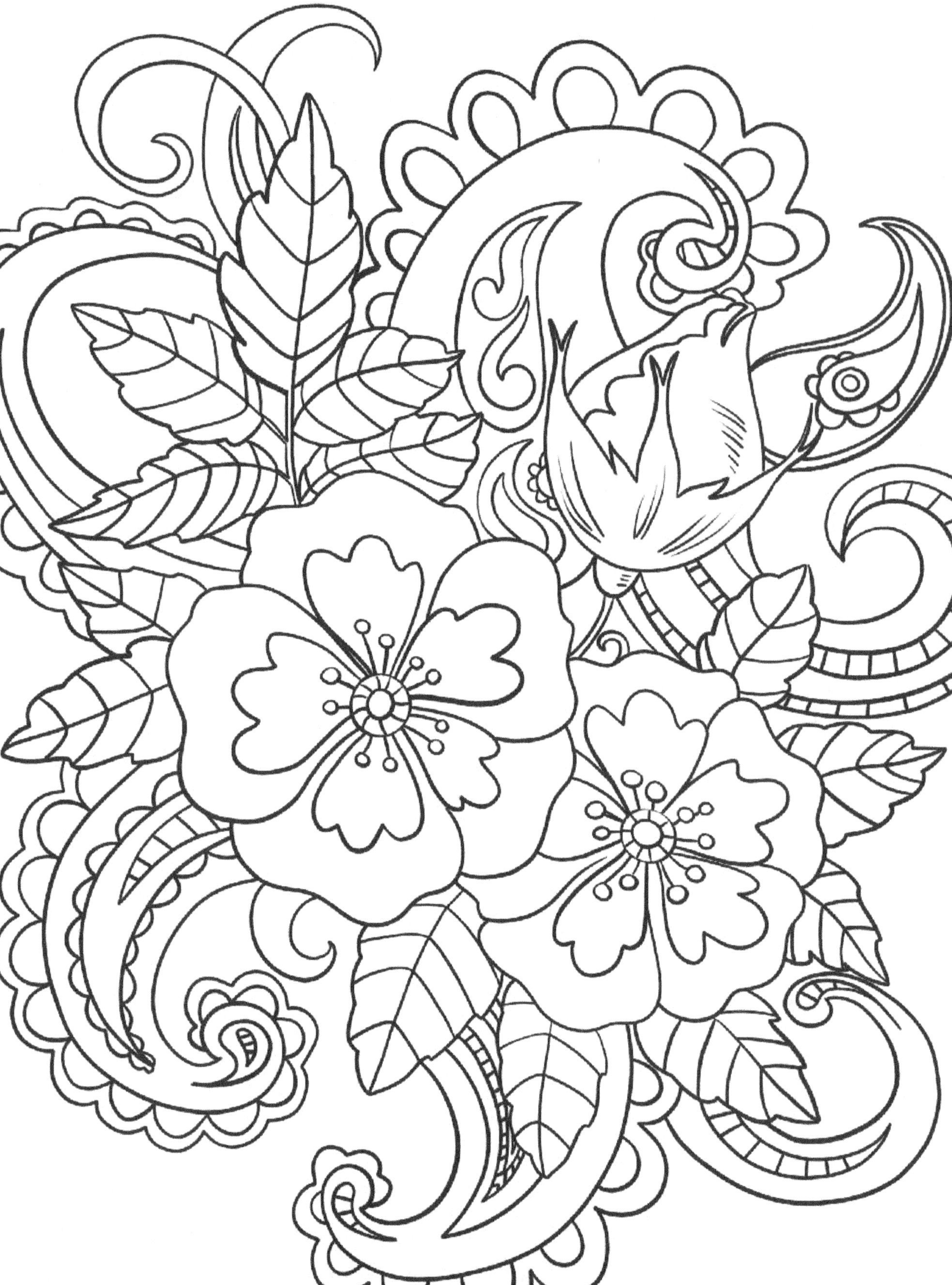

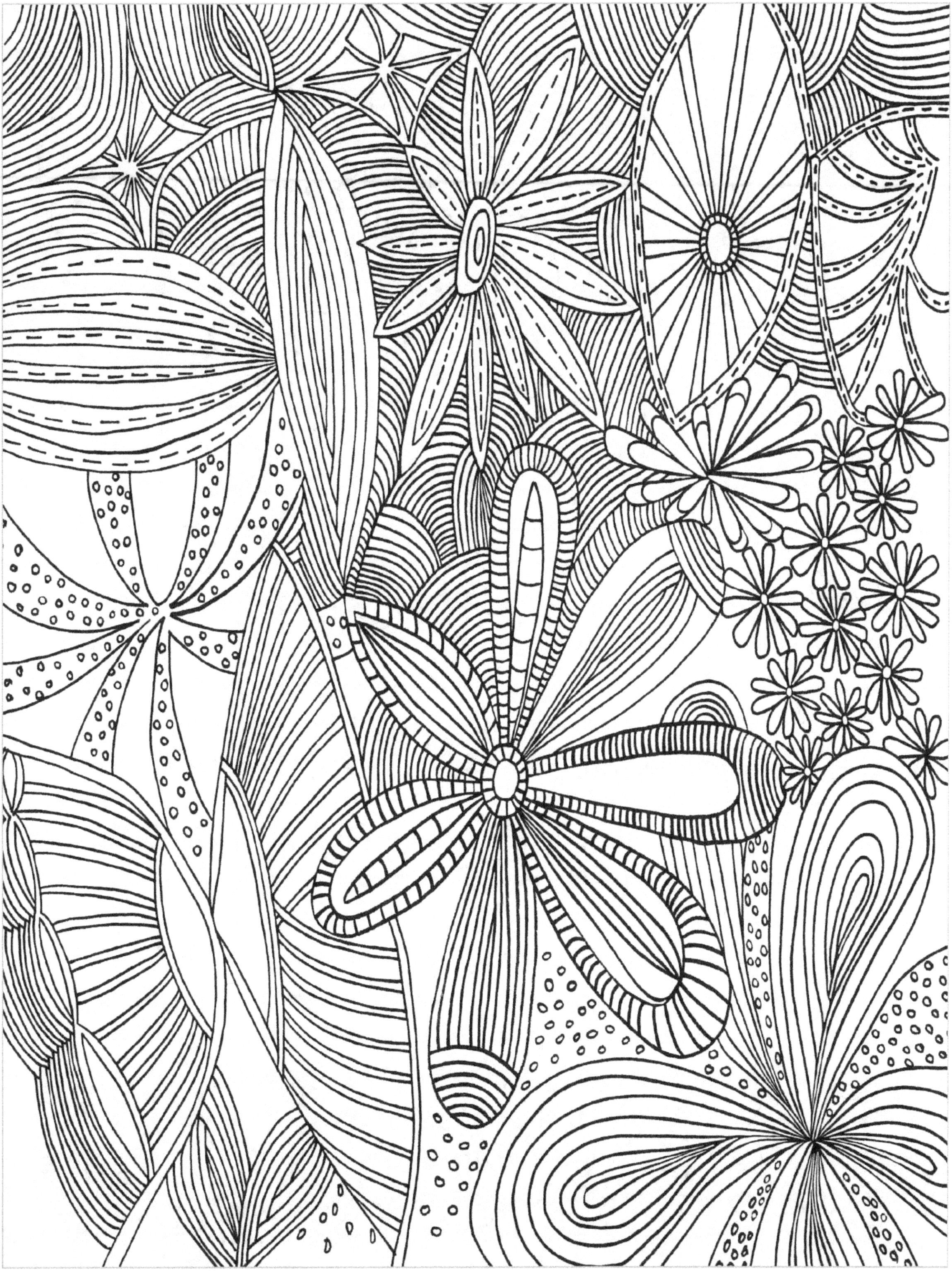

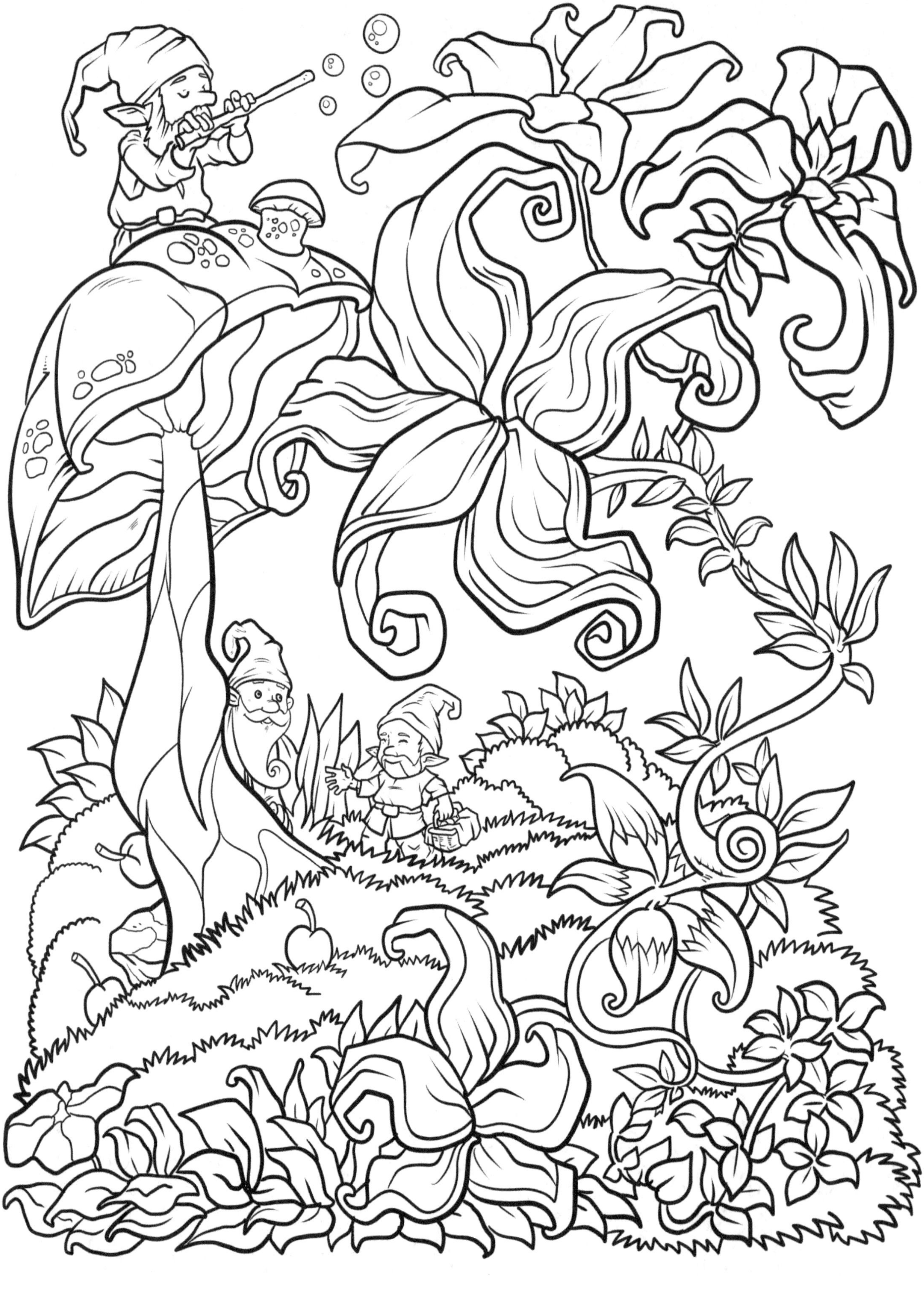

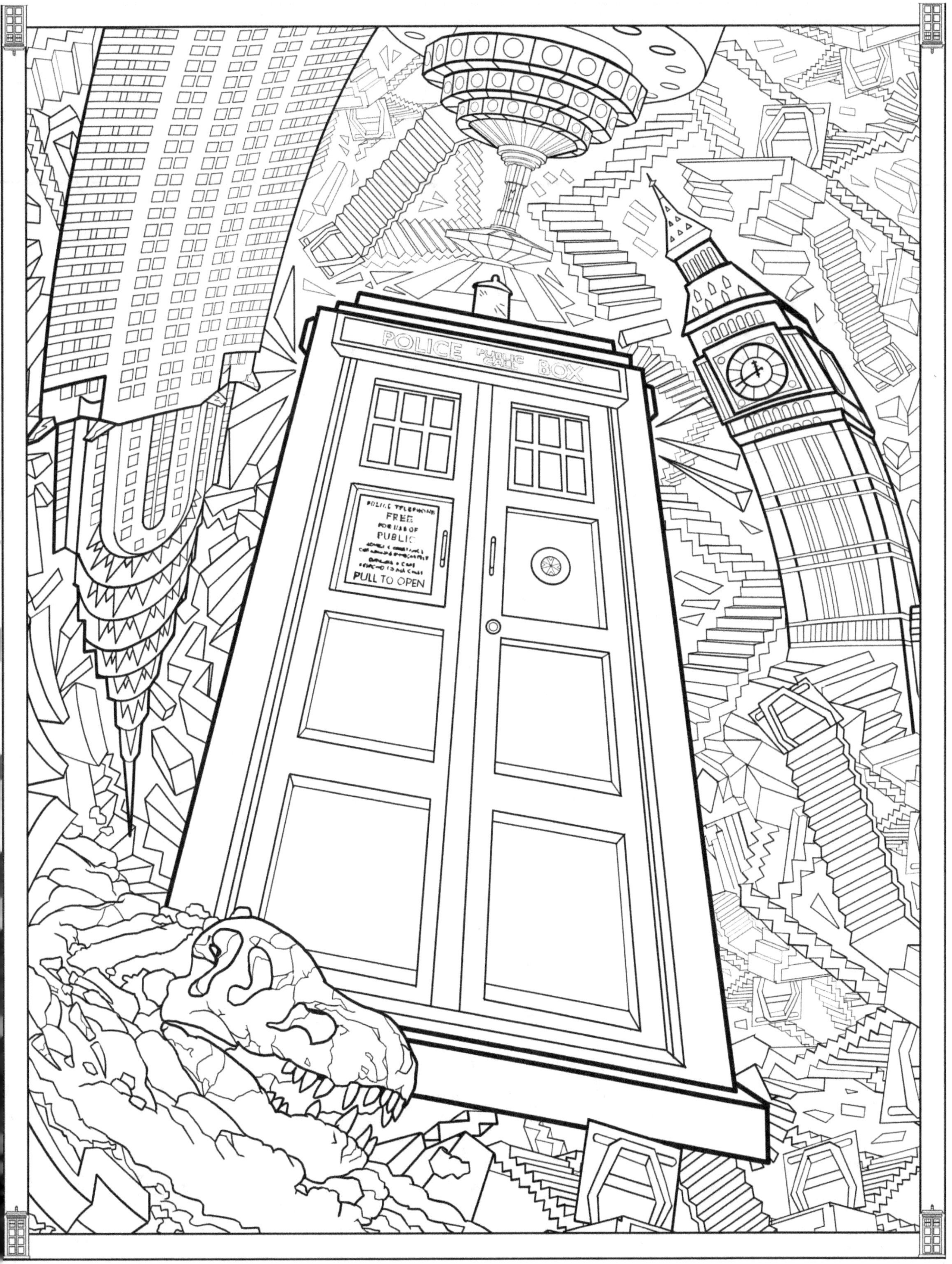
POLICE PUBLIC CALL BOX
POLICE TELEPHONE
FREE
FOR USE OF
PUBLIC
PULL TO OPEN

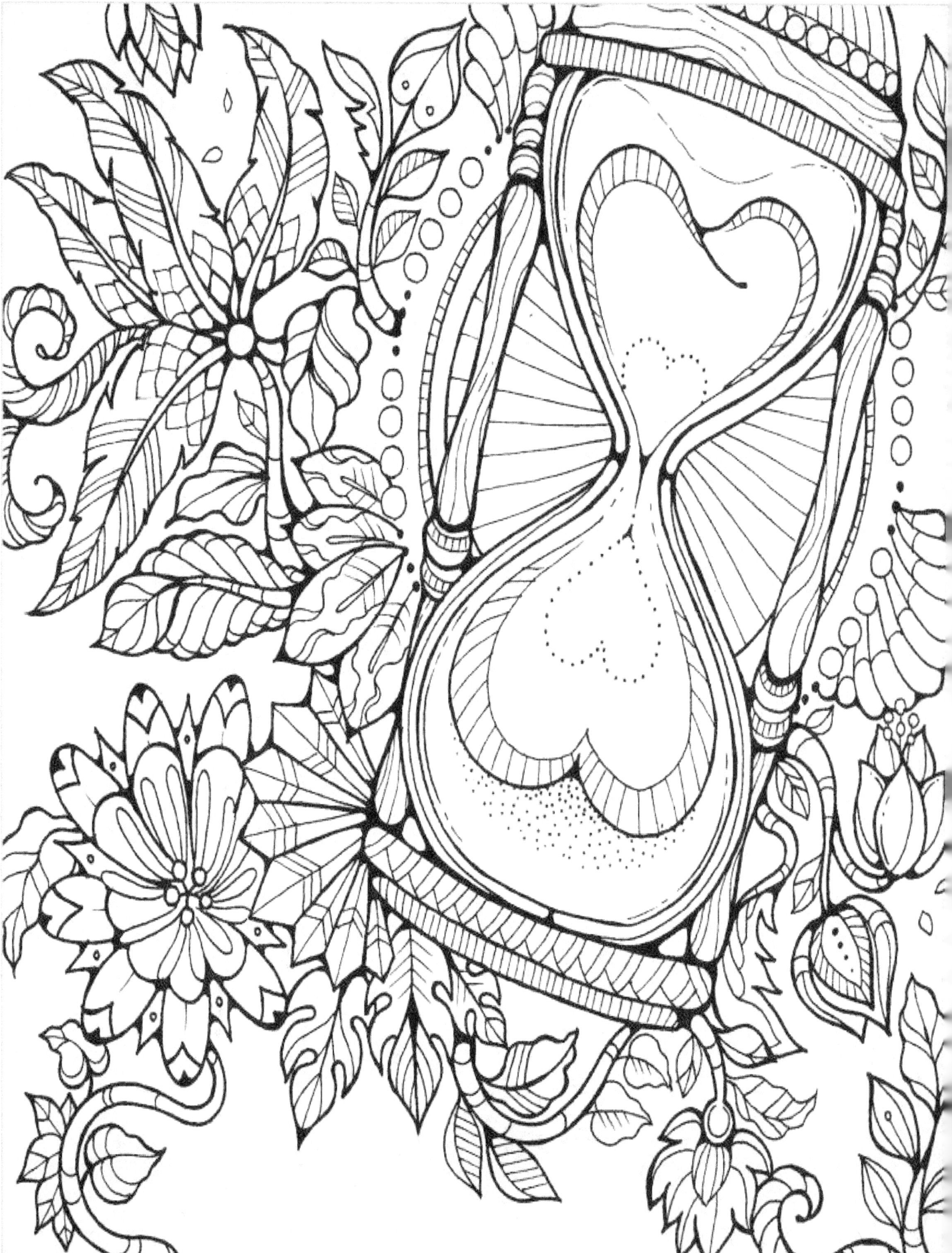

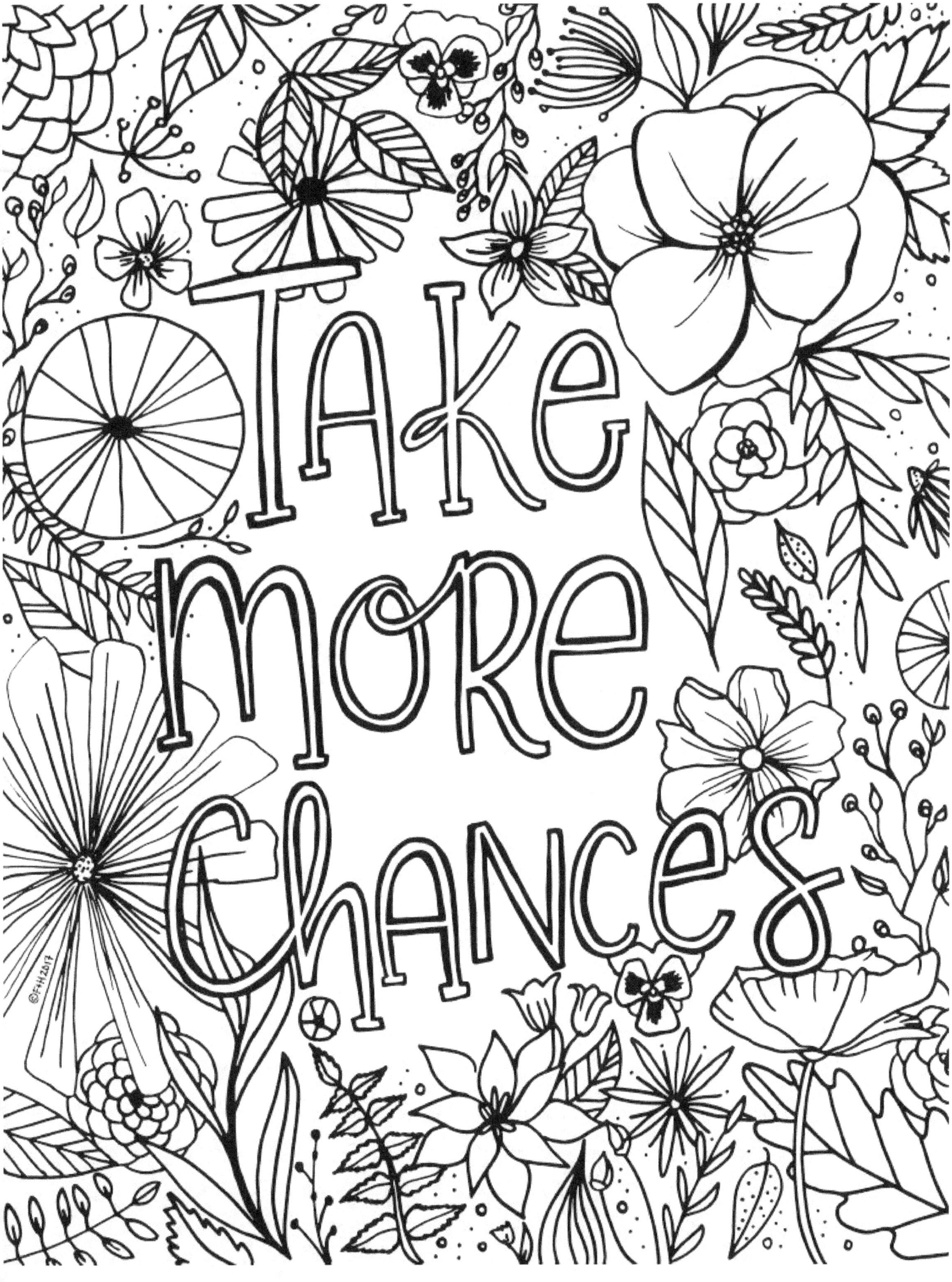
Take
more
Chances
©F+H2017

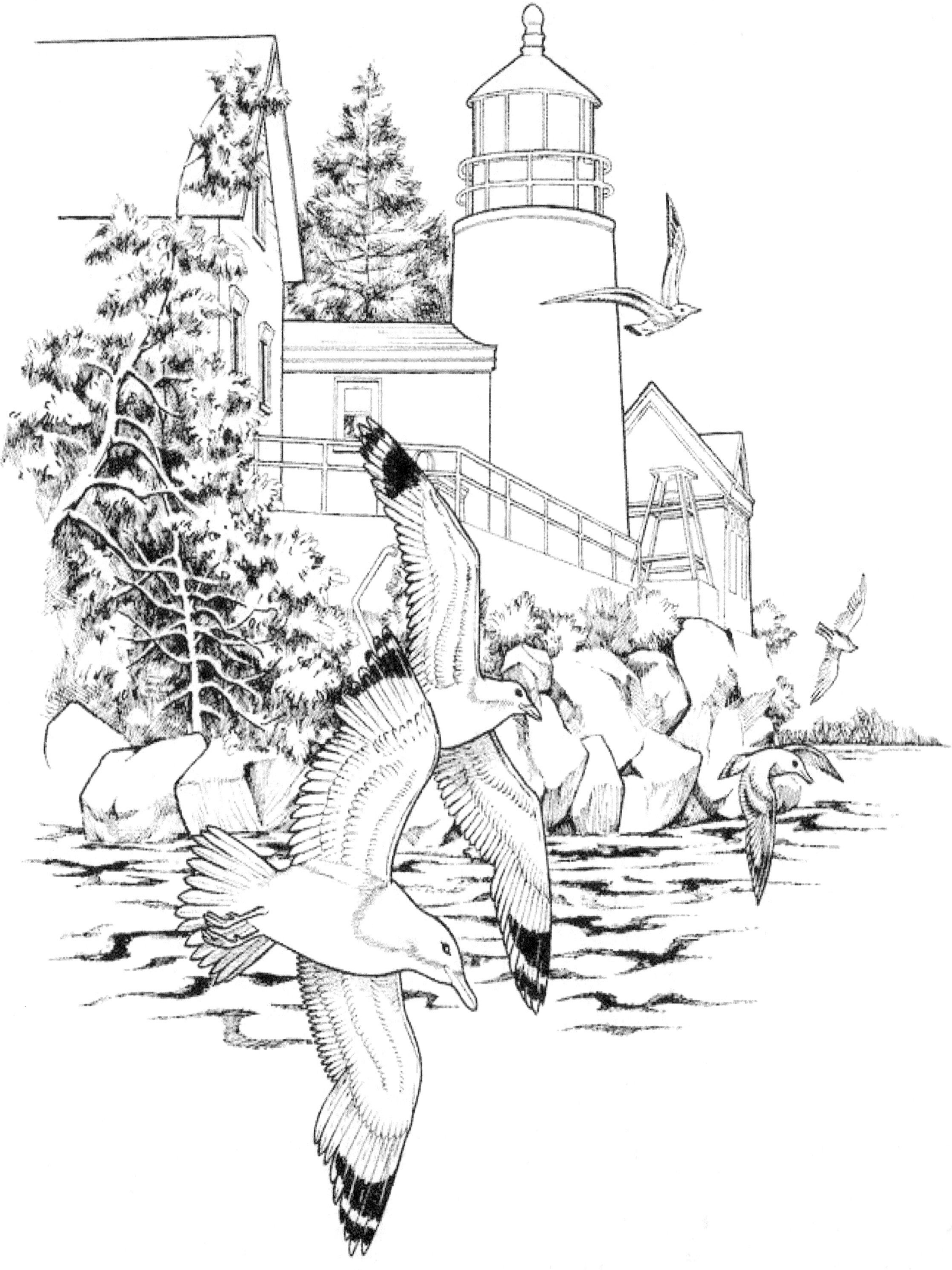

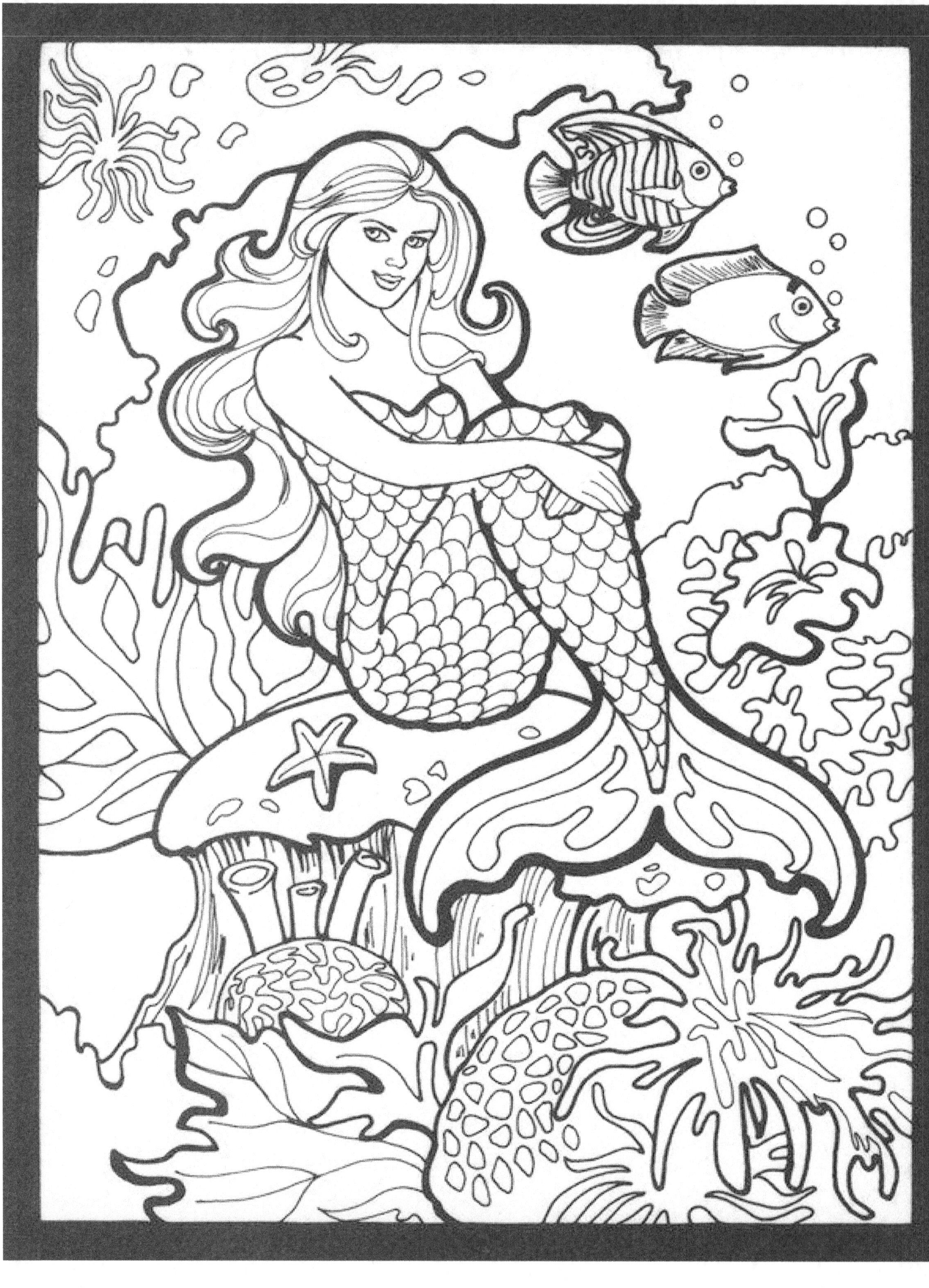

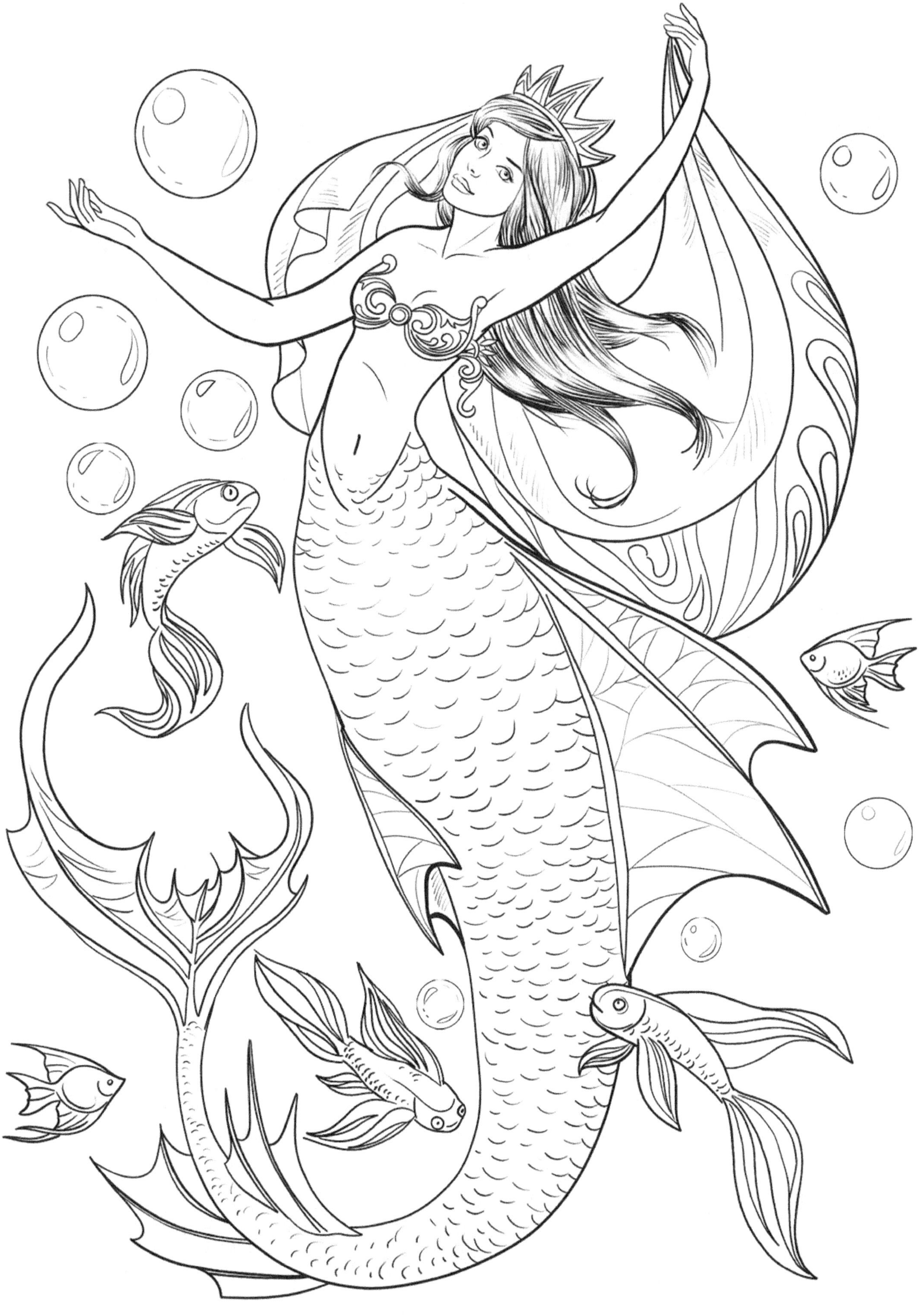

Petunia

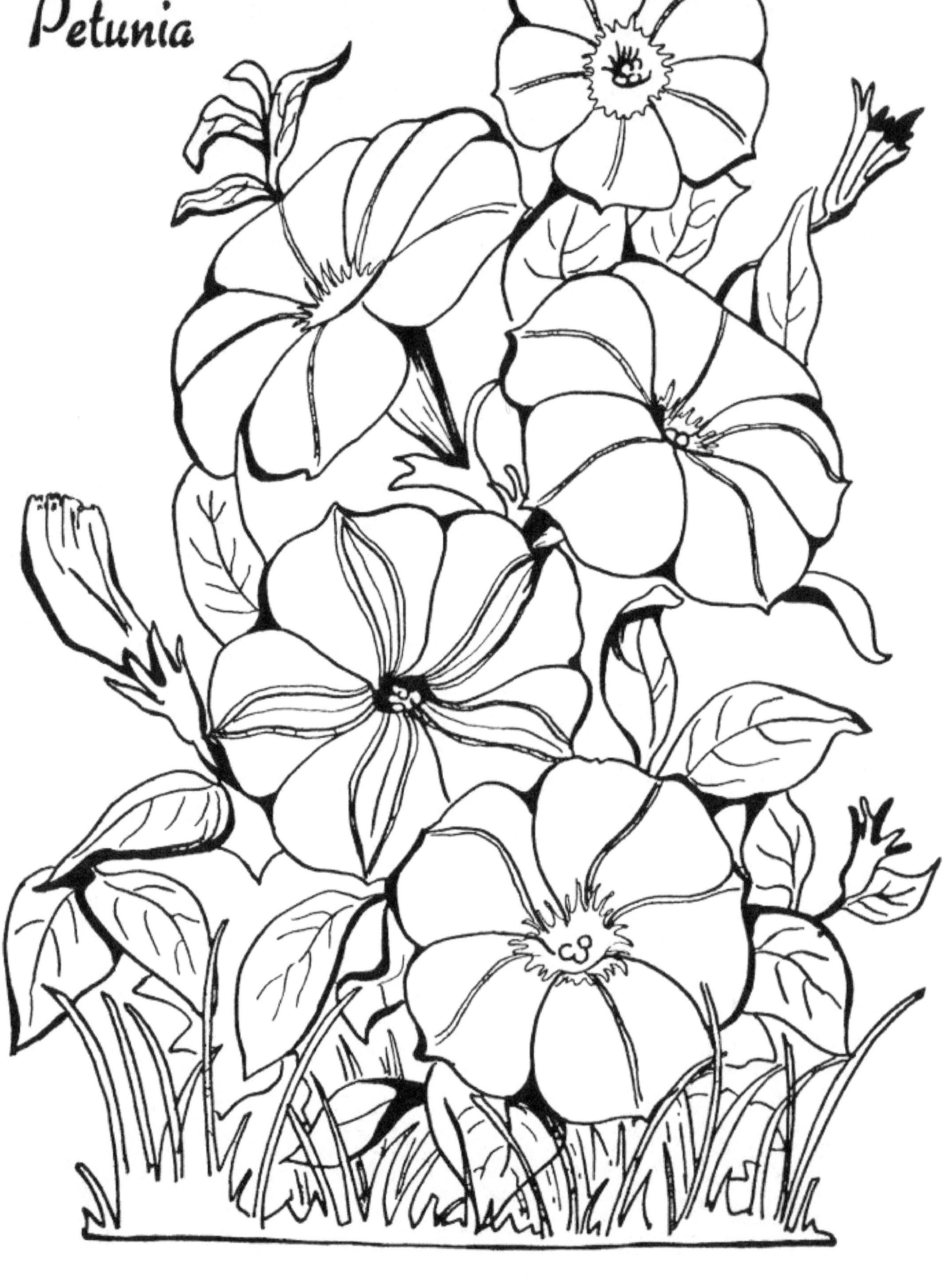

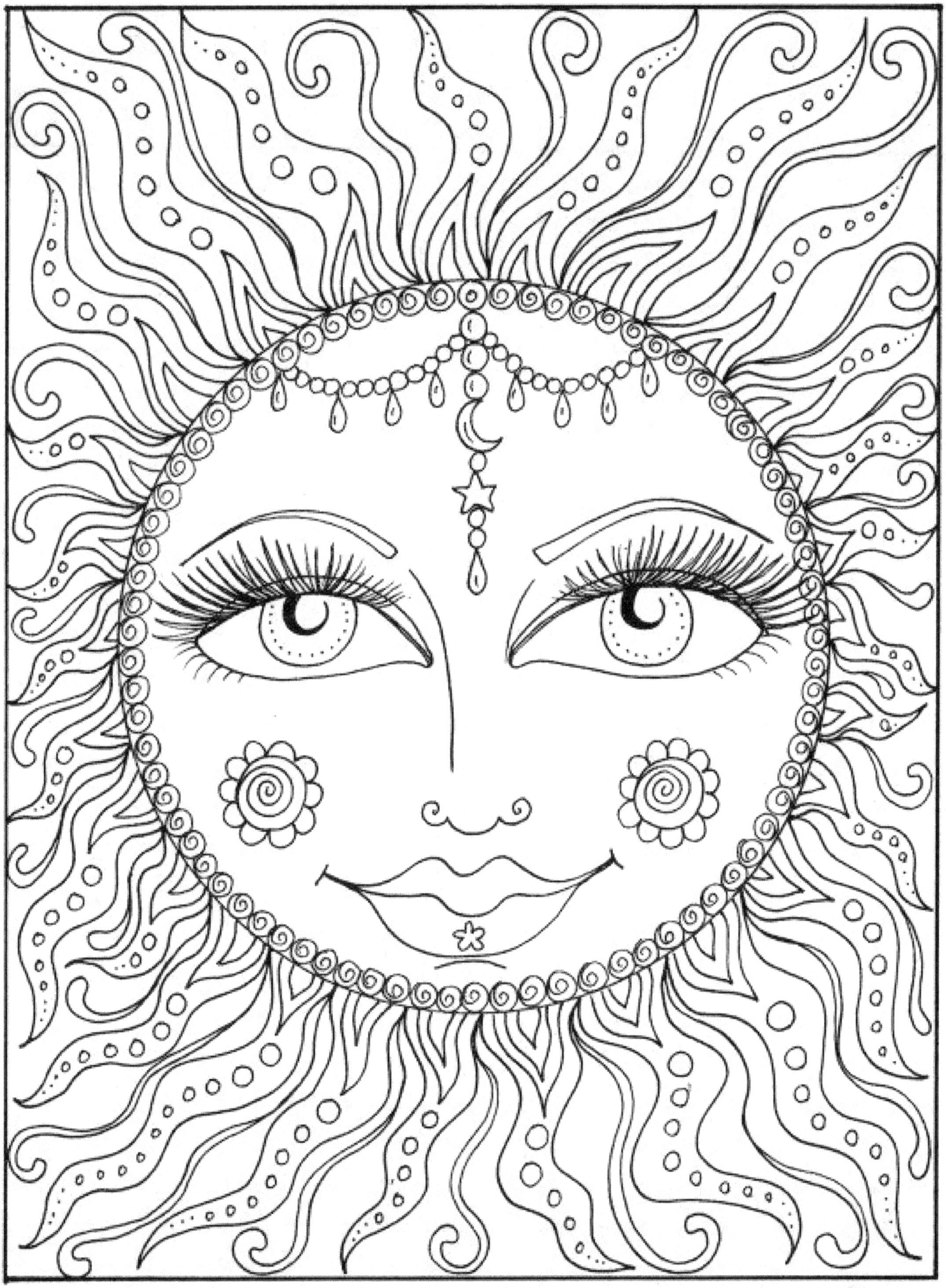

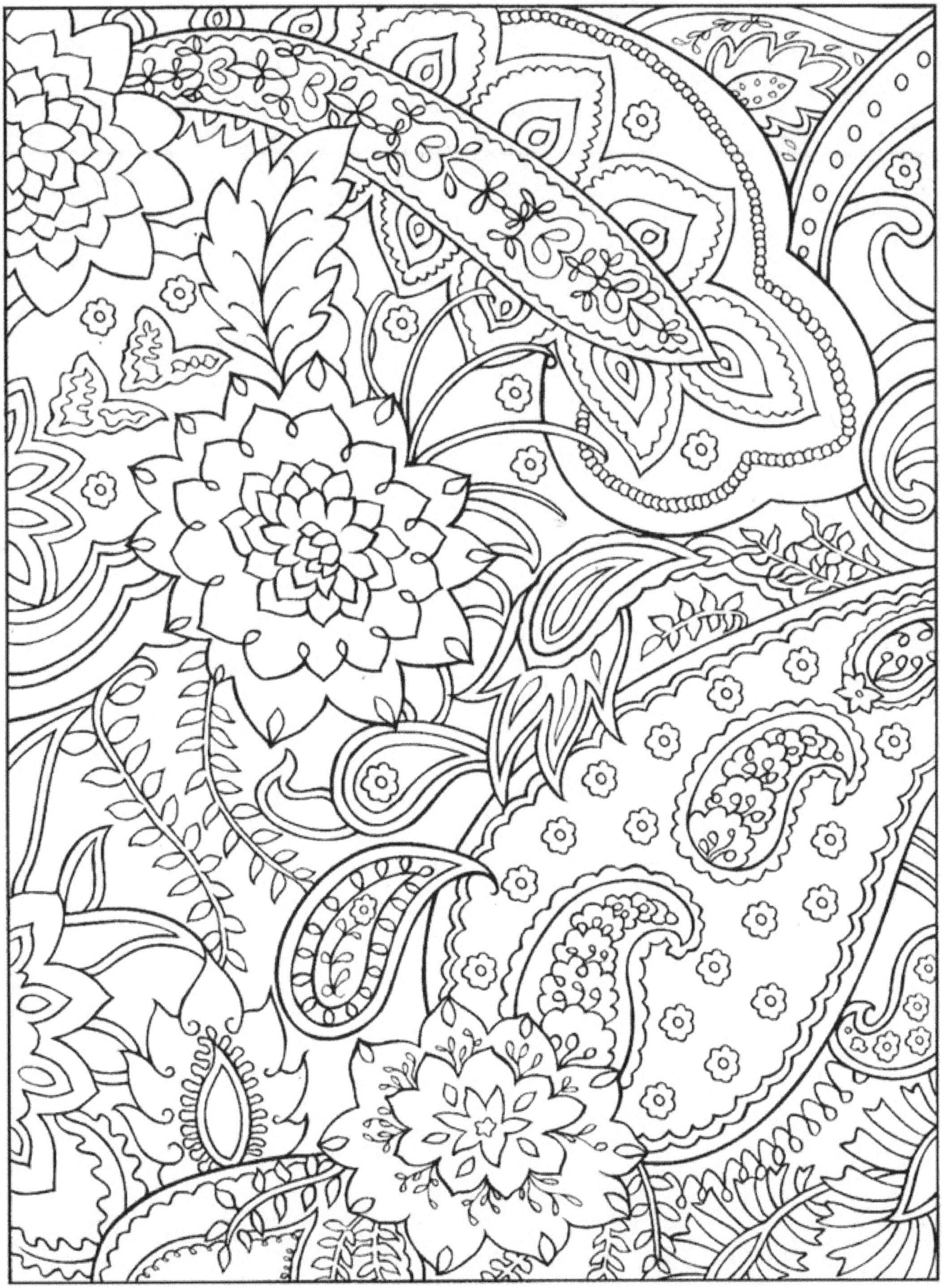

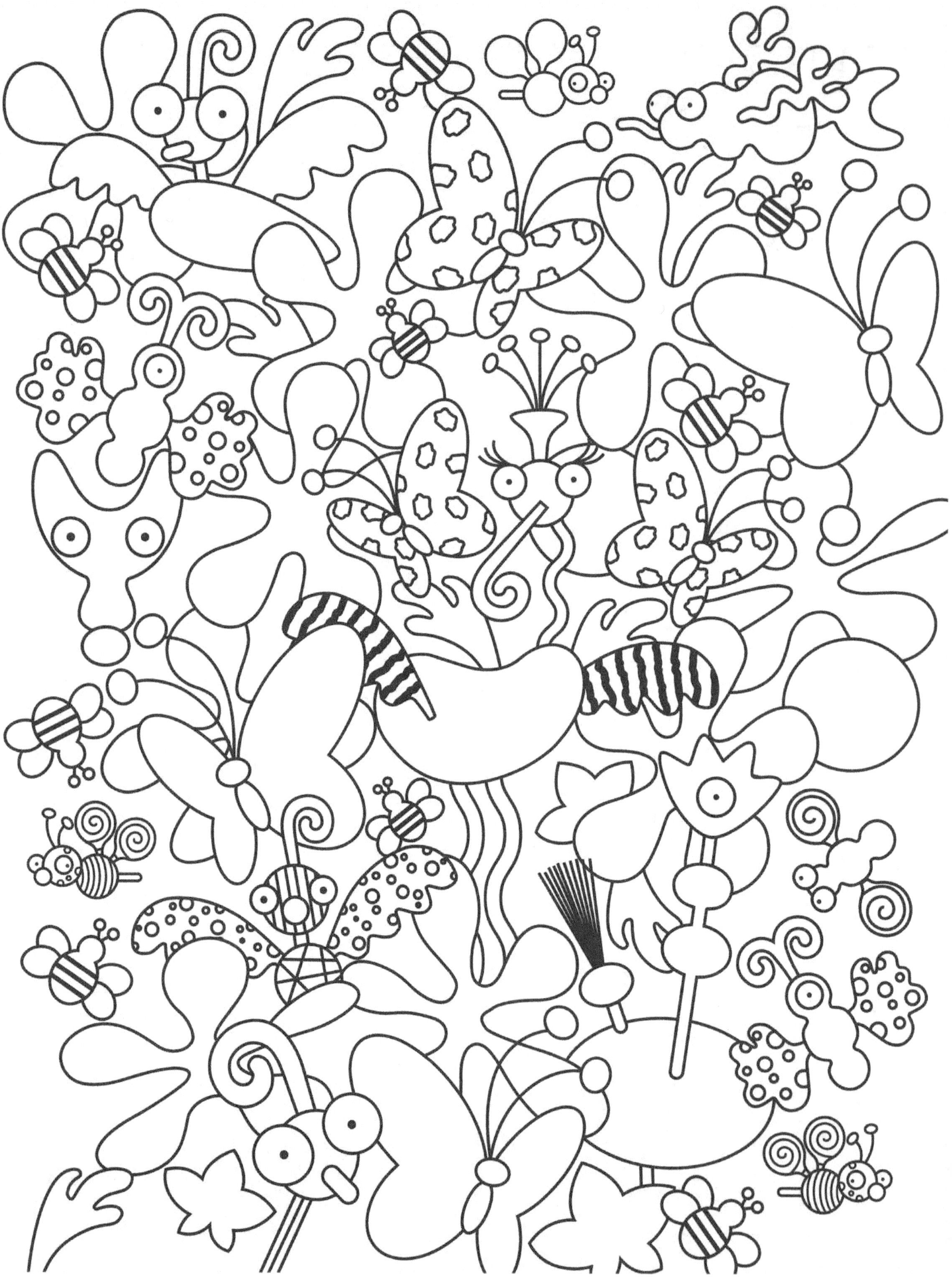

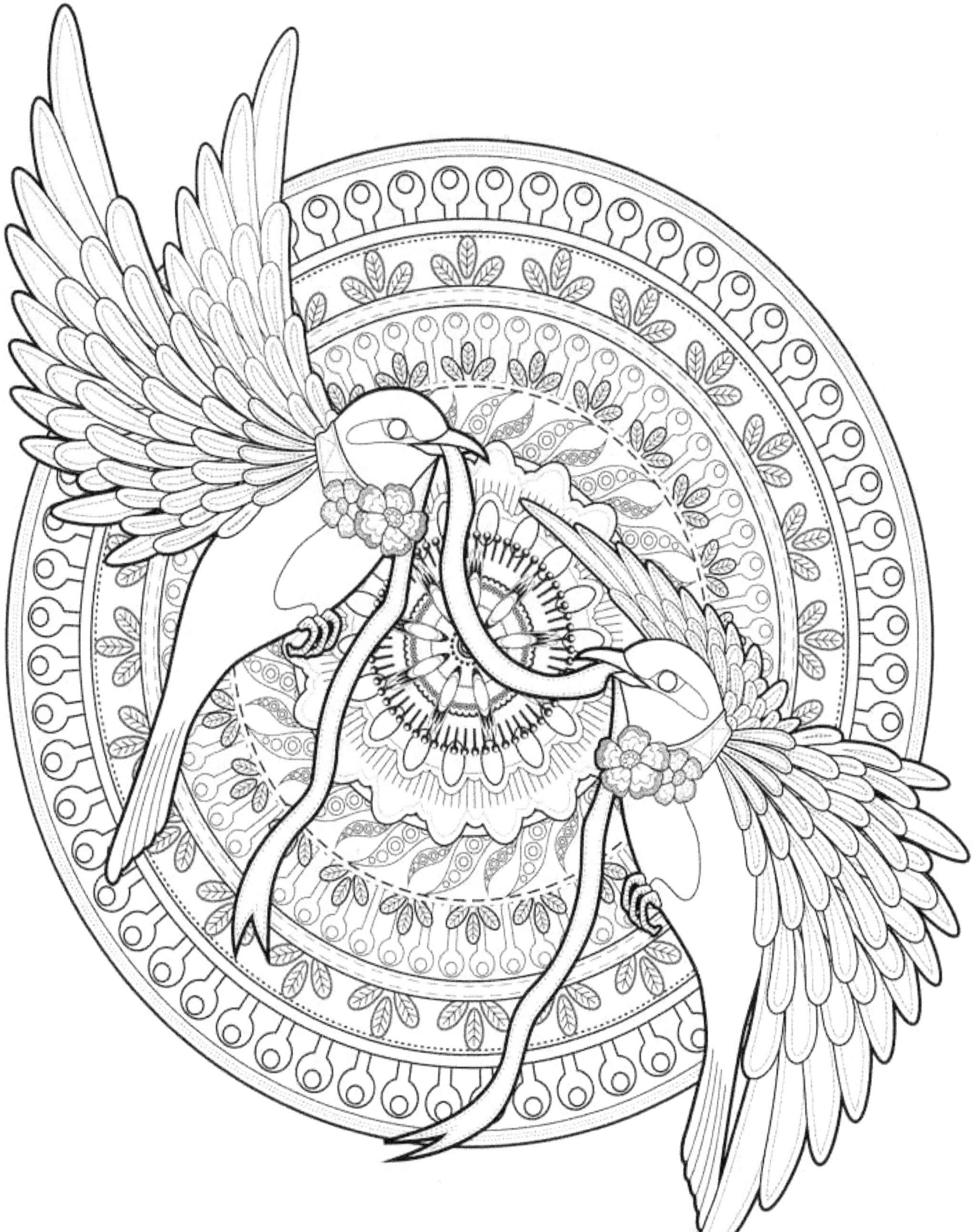

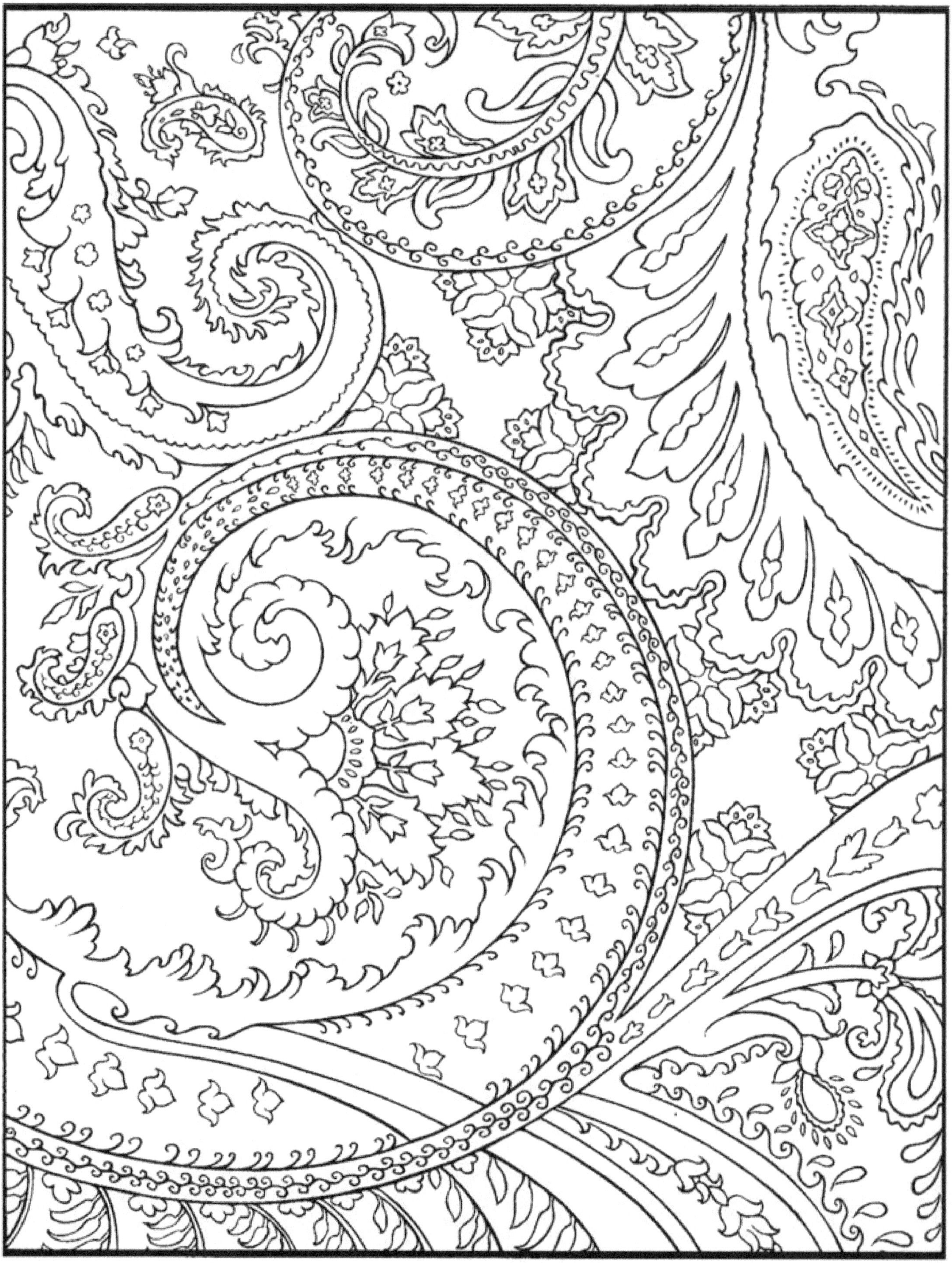

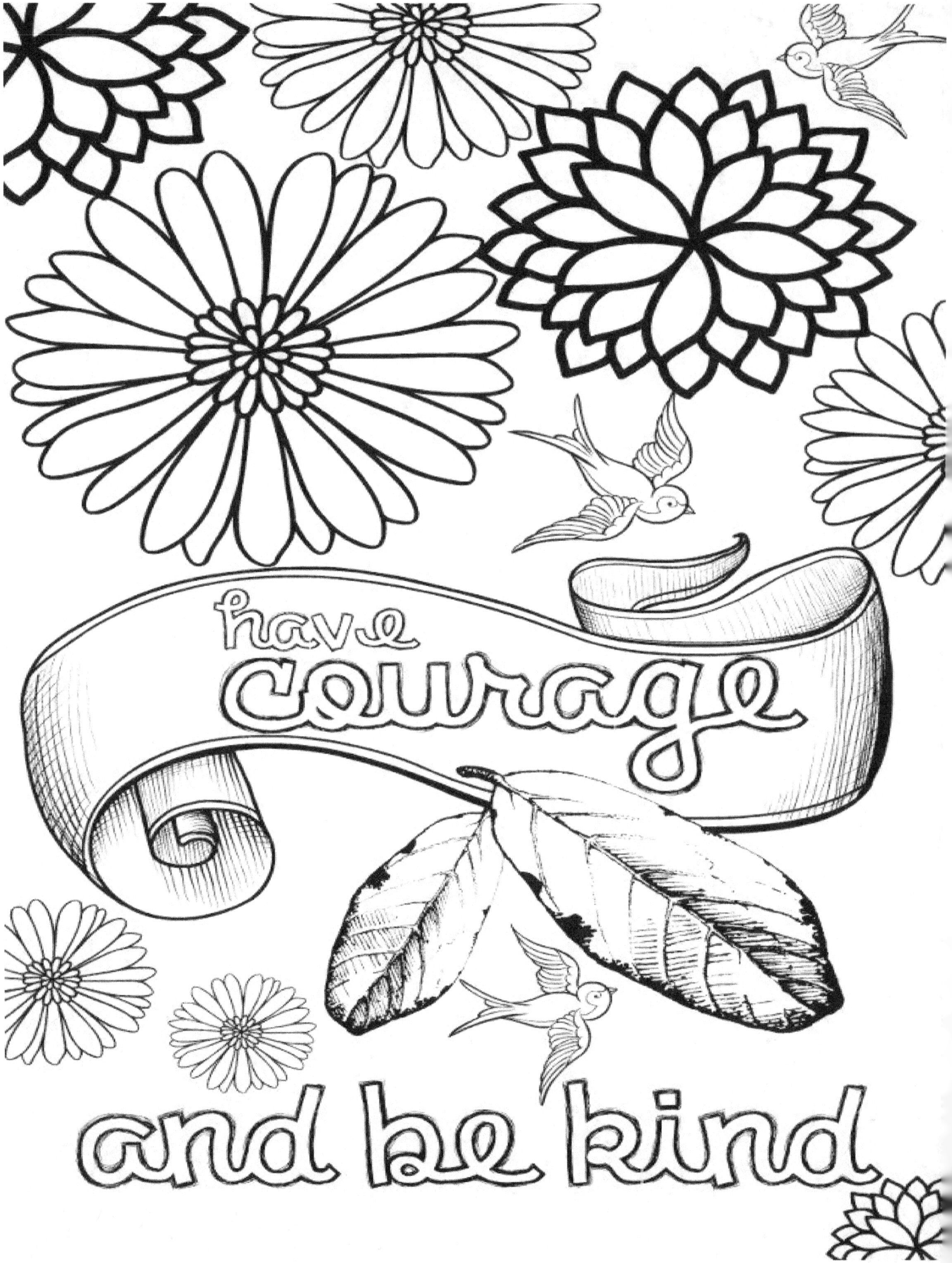
have courage
and be kind

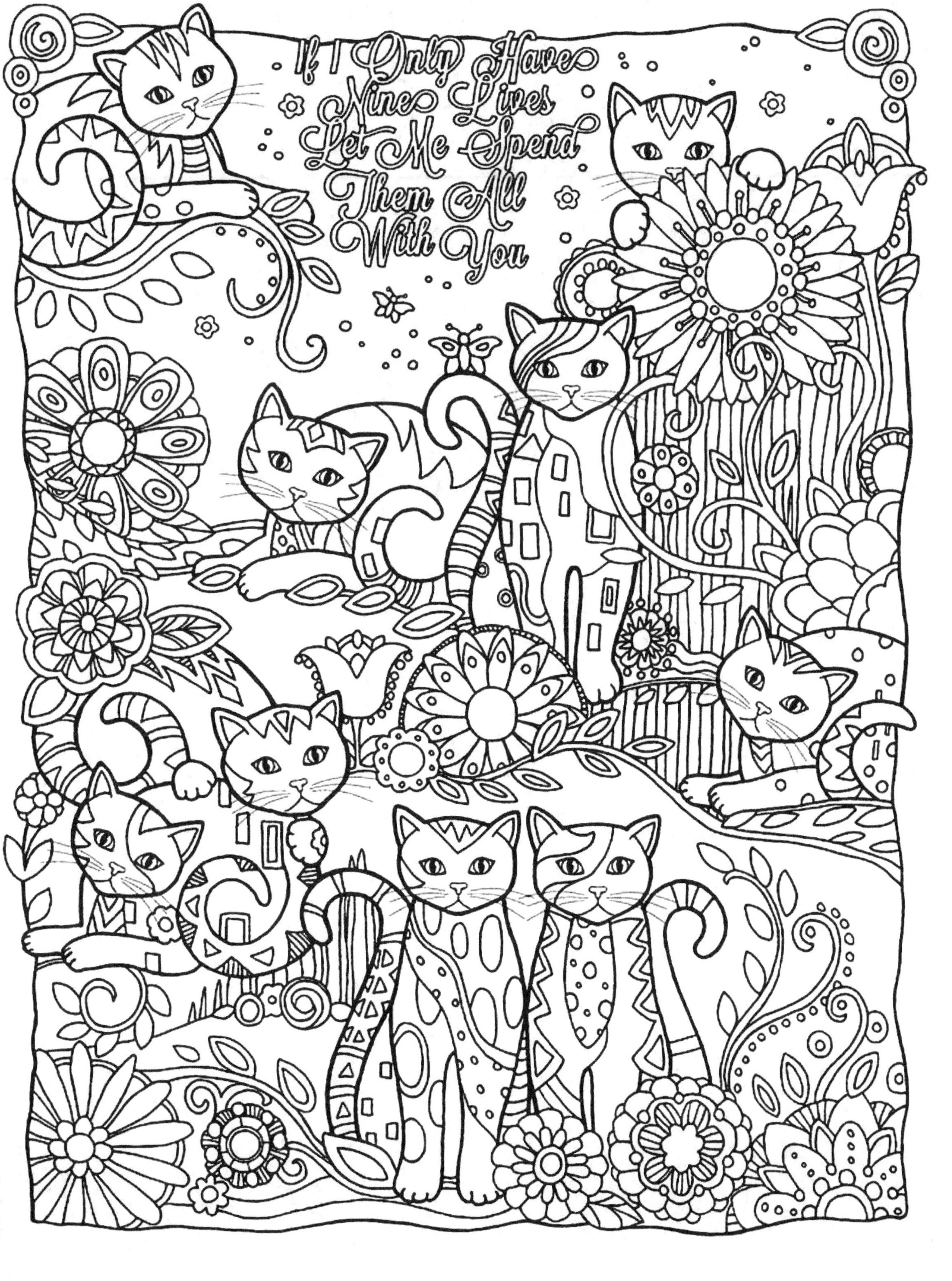
If I Only Have Nine Lives Let Me Spend Them All With You

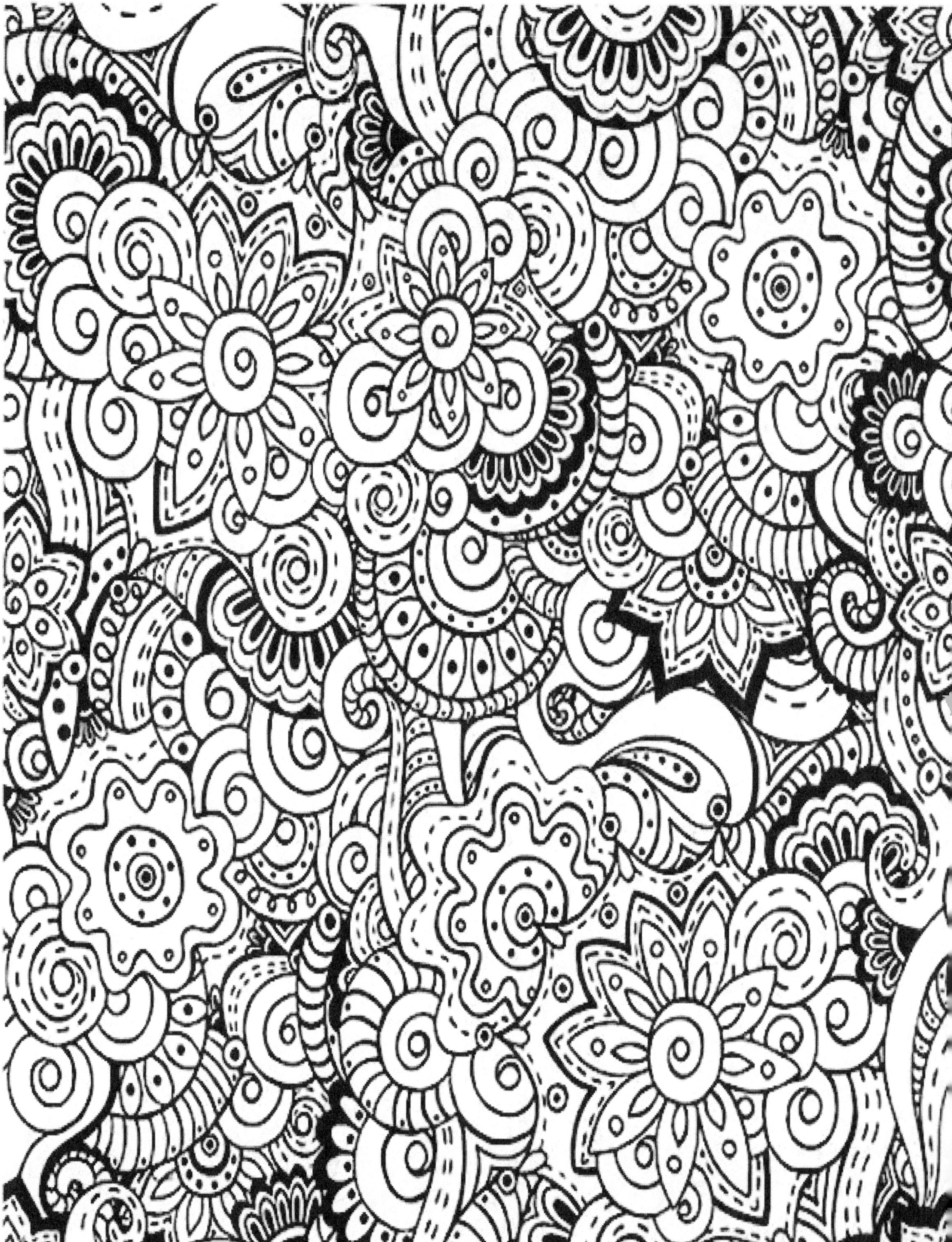

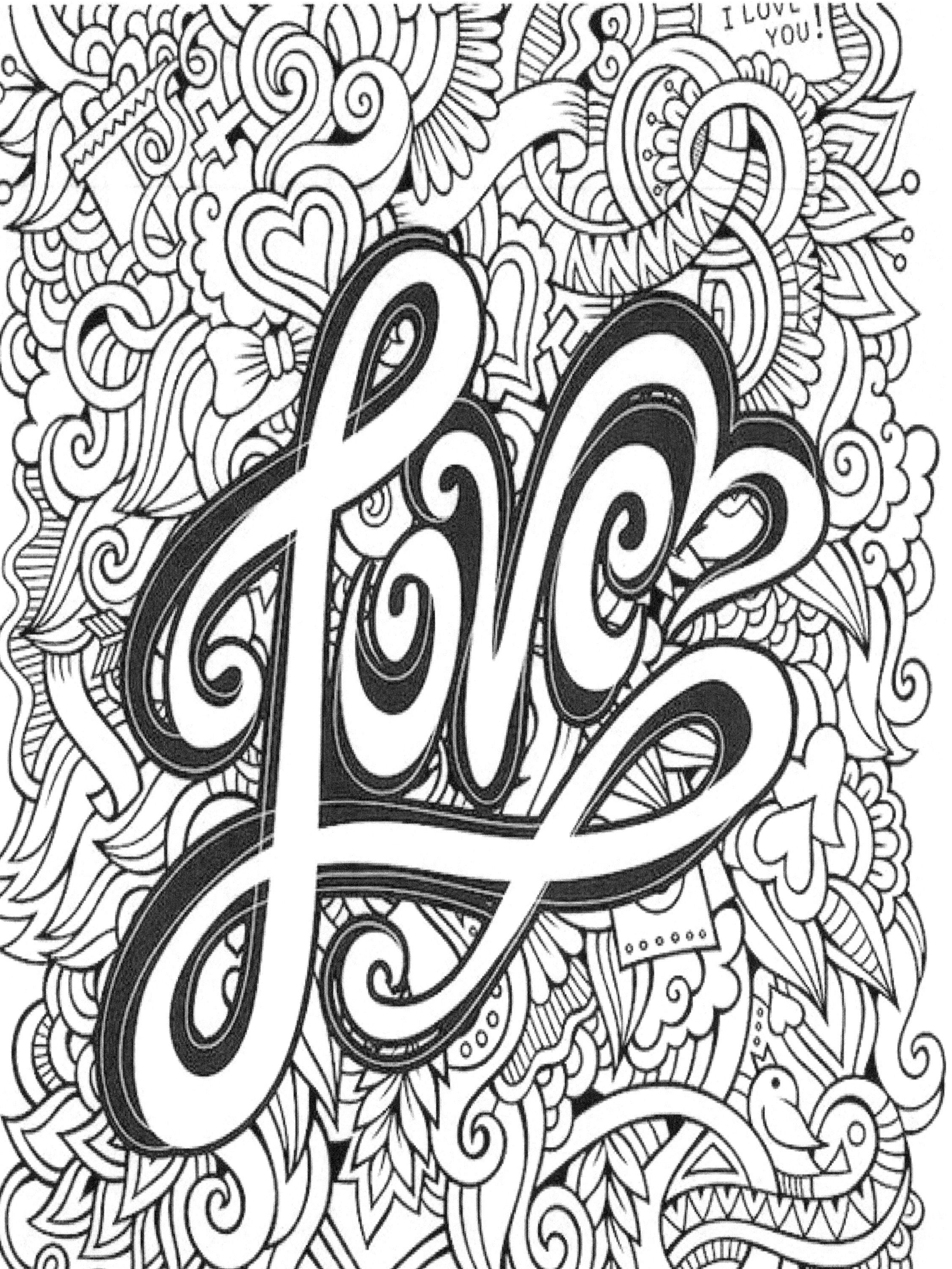
I LOVE YOU!
Love

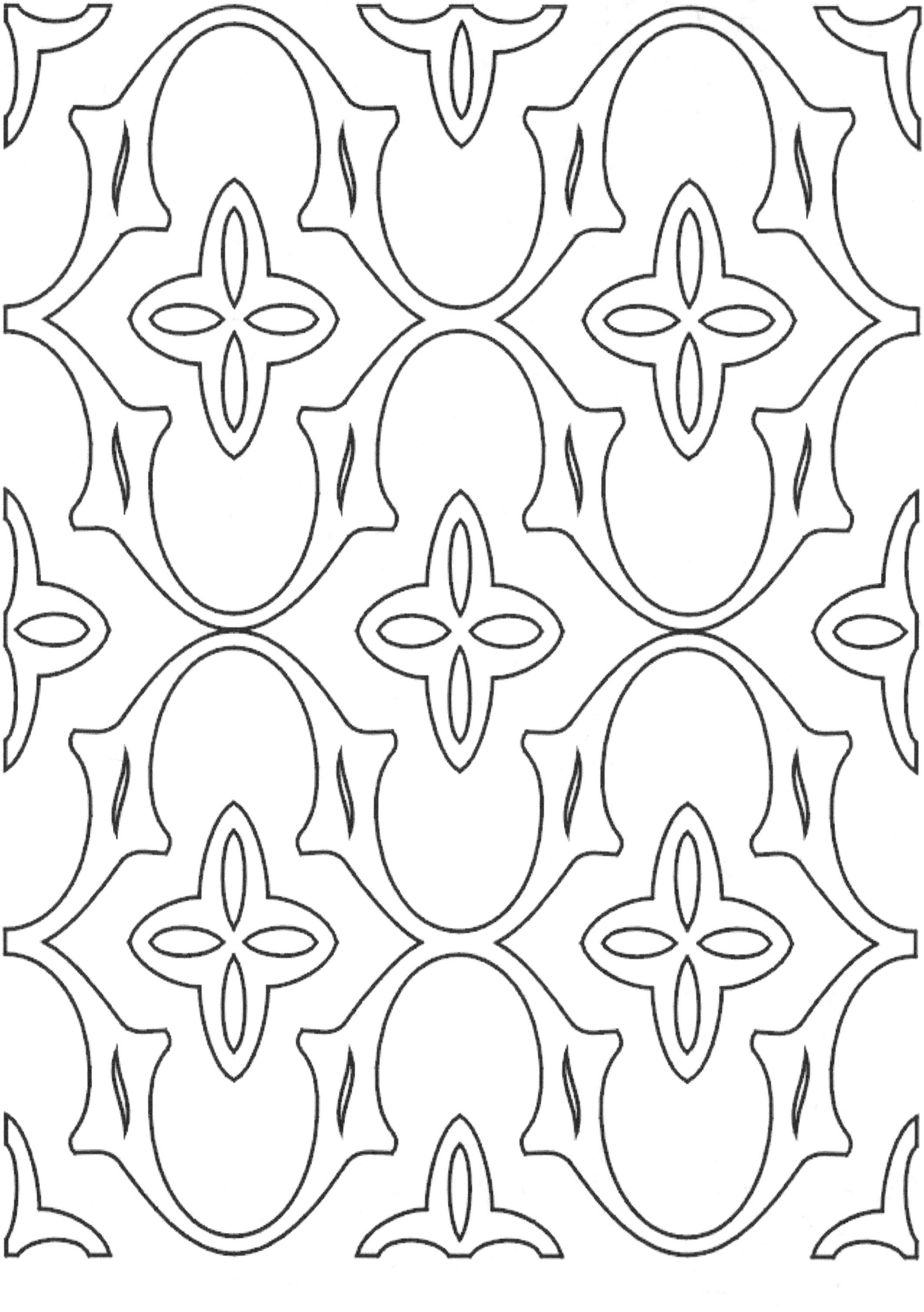

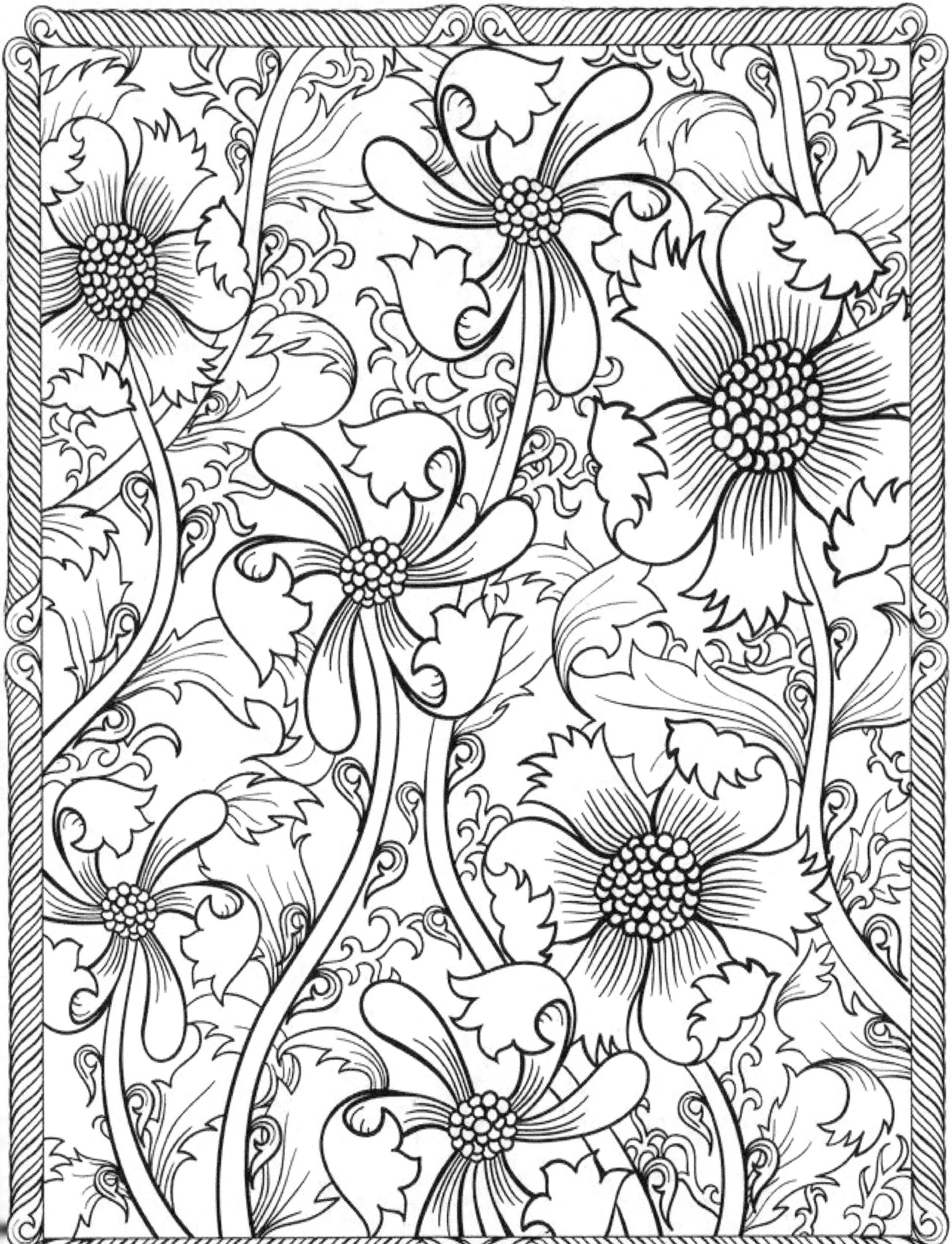

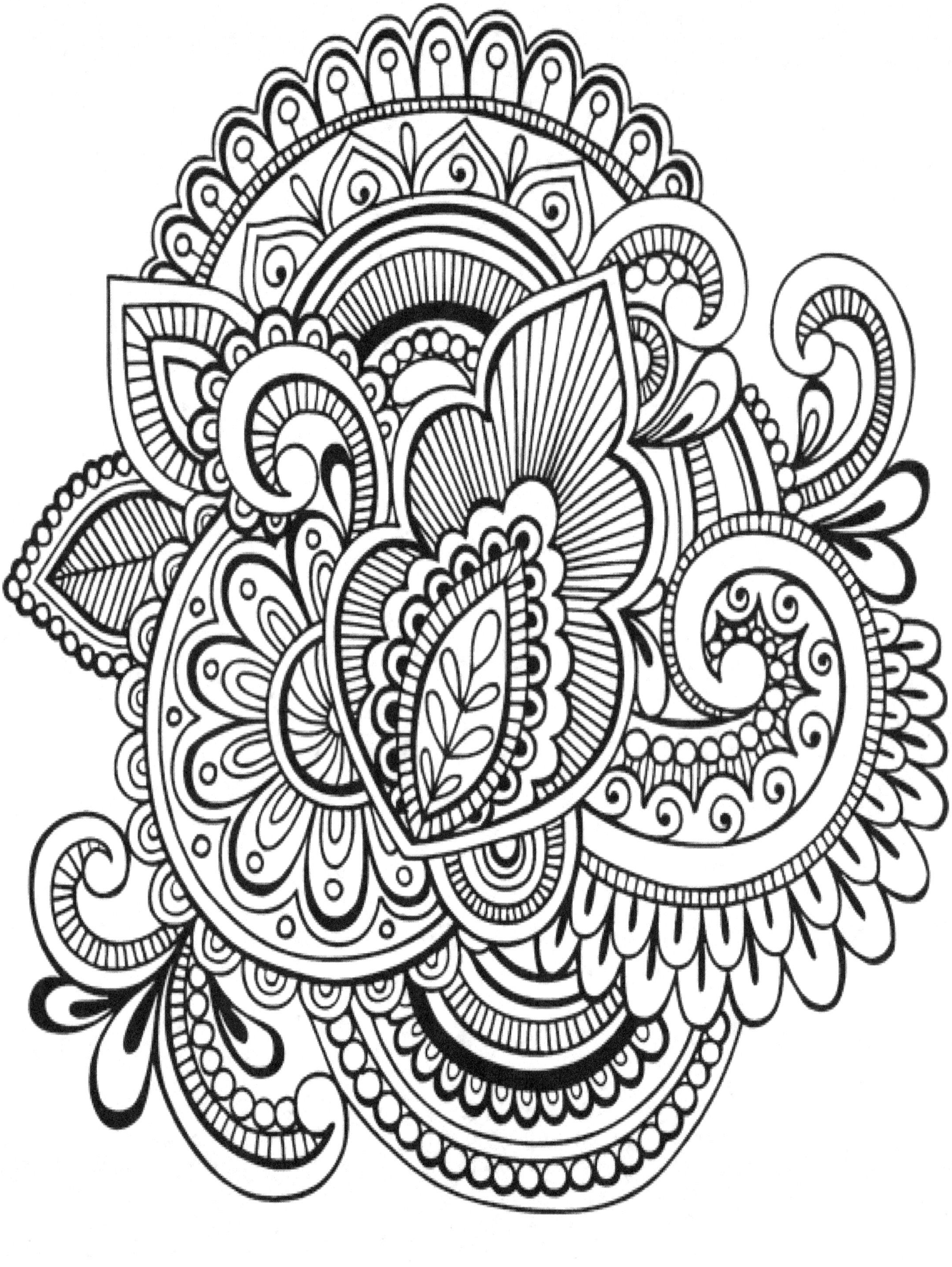

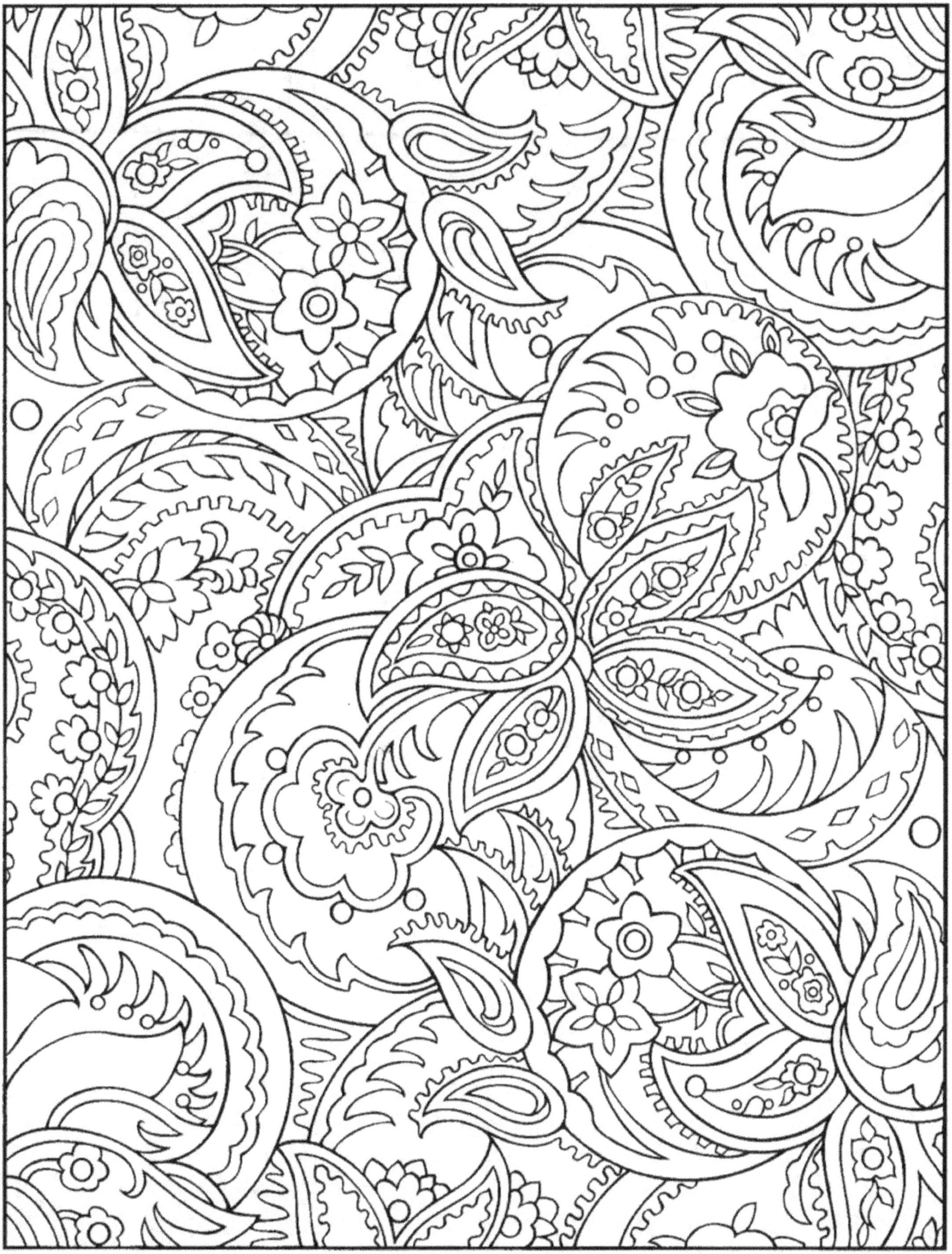

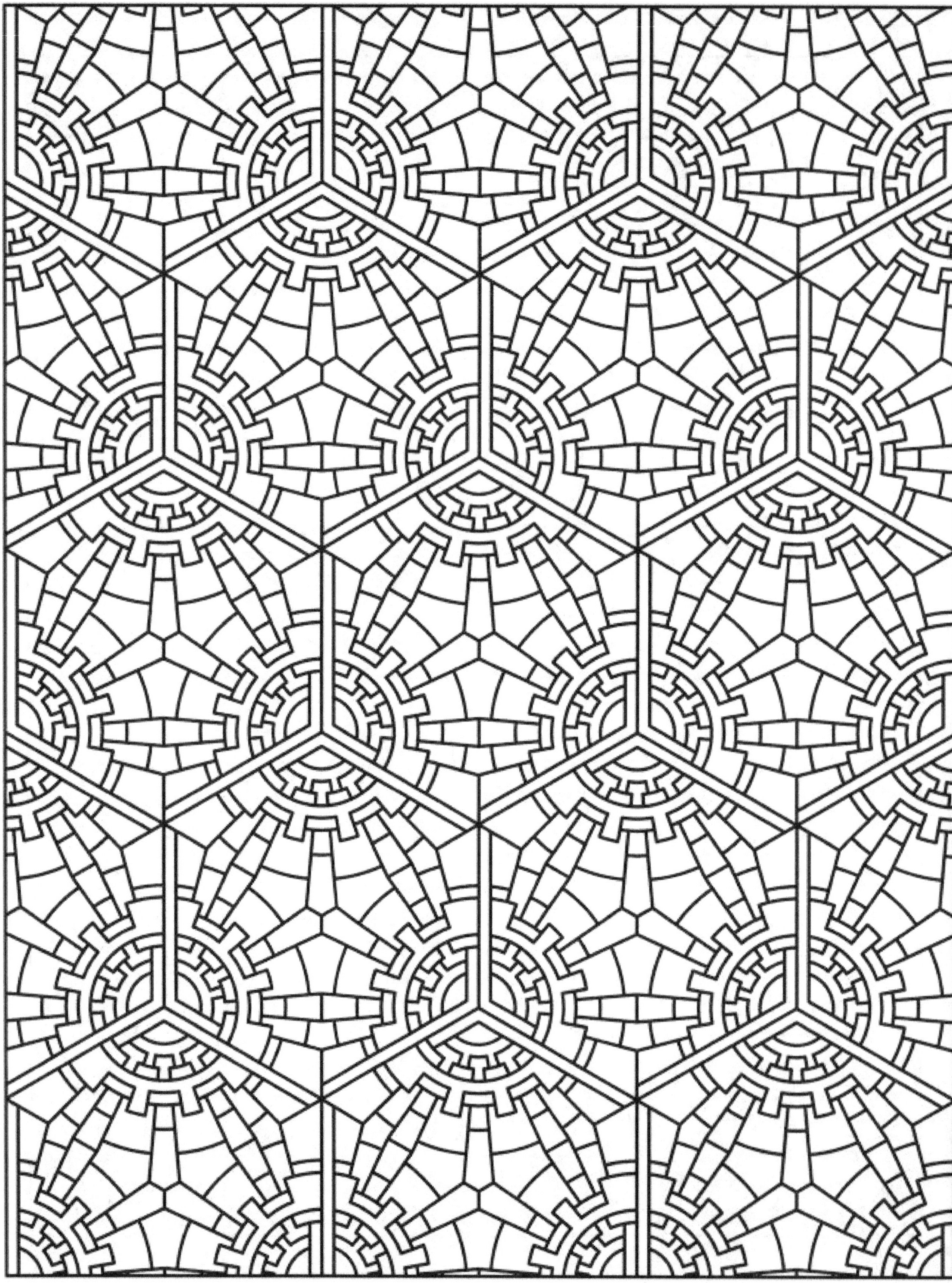

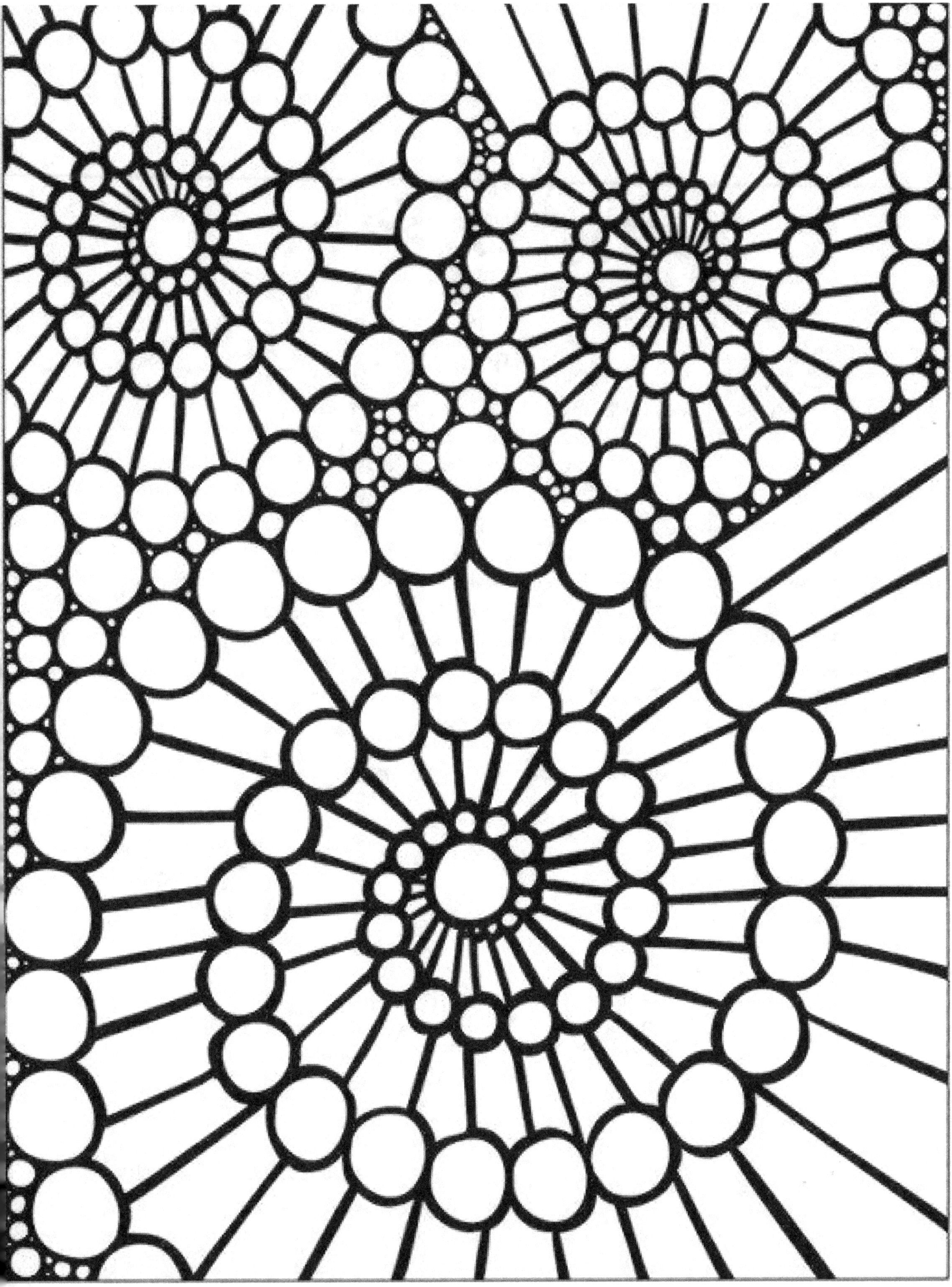

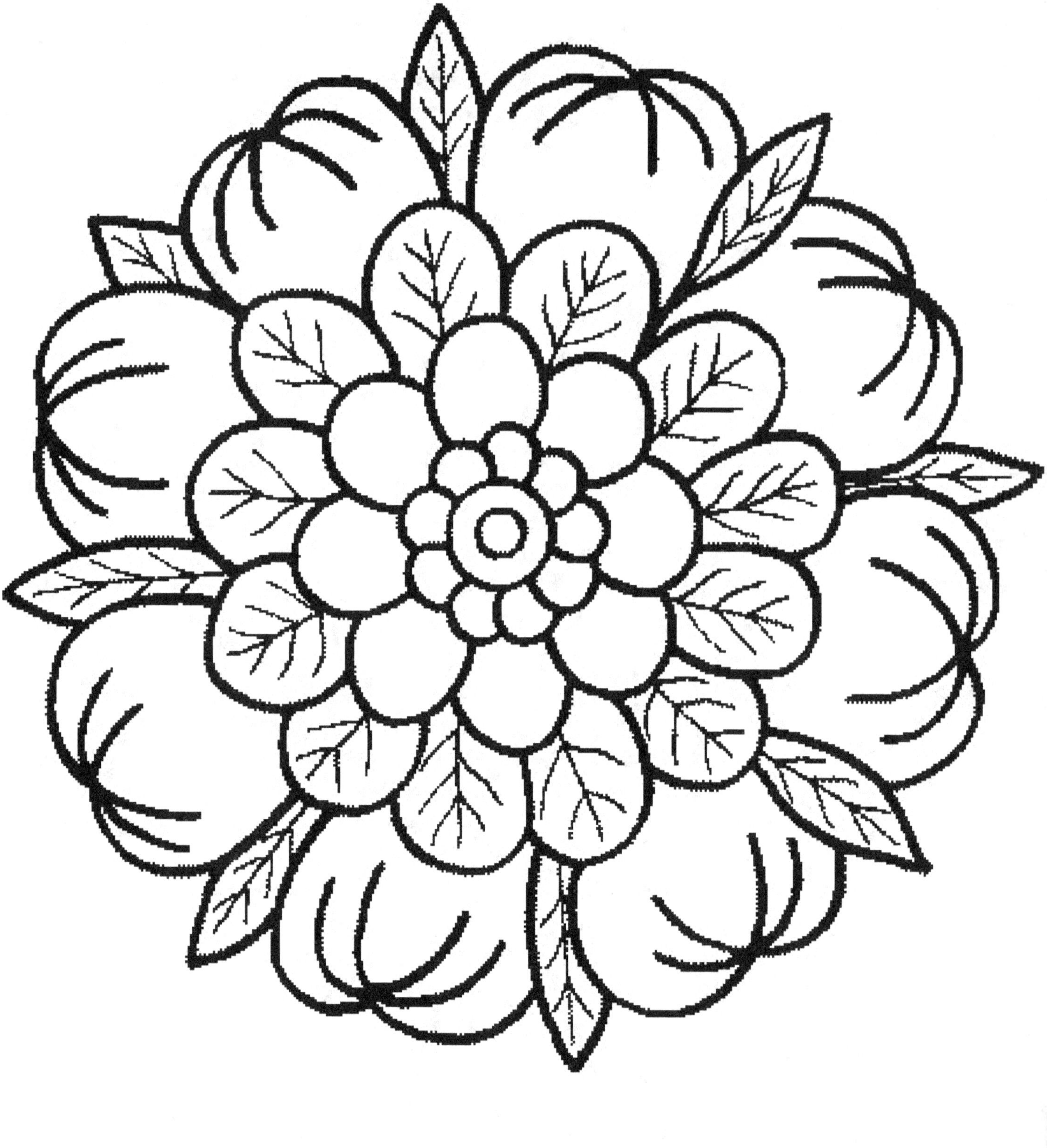

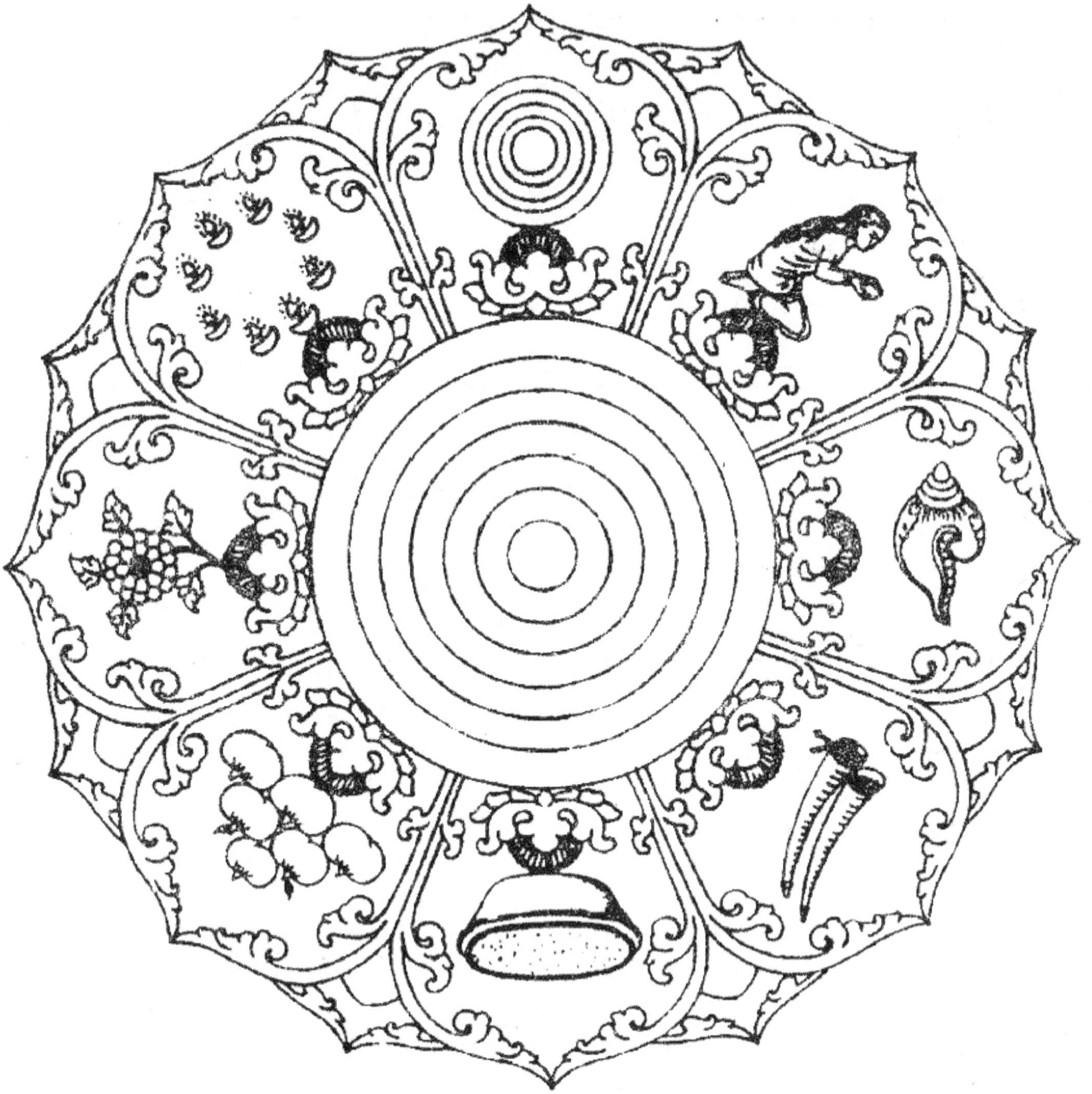

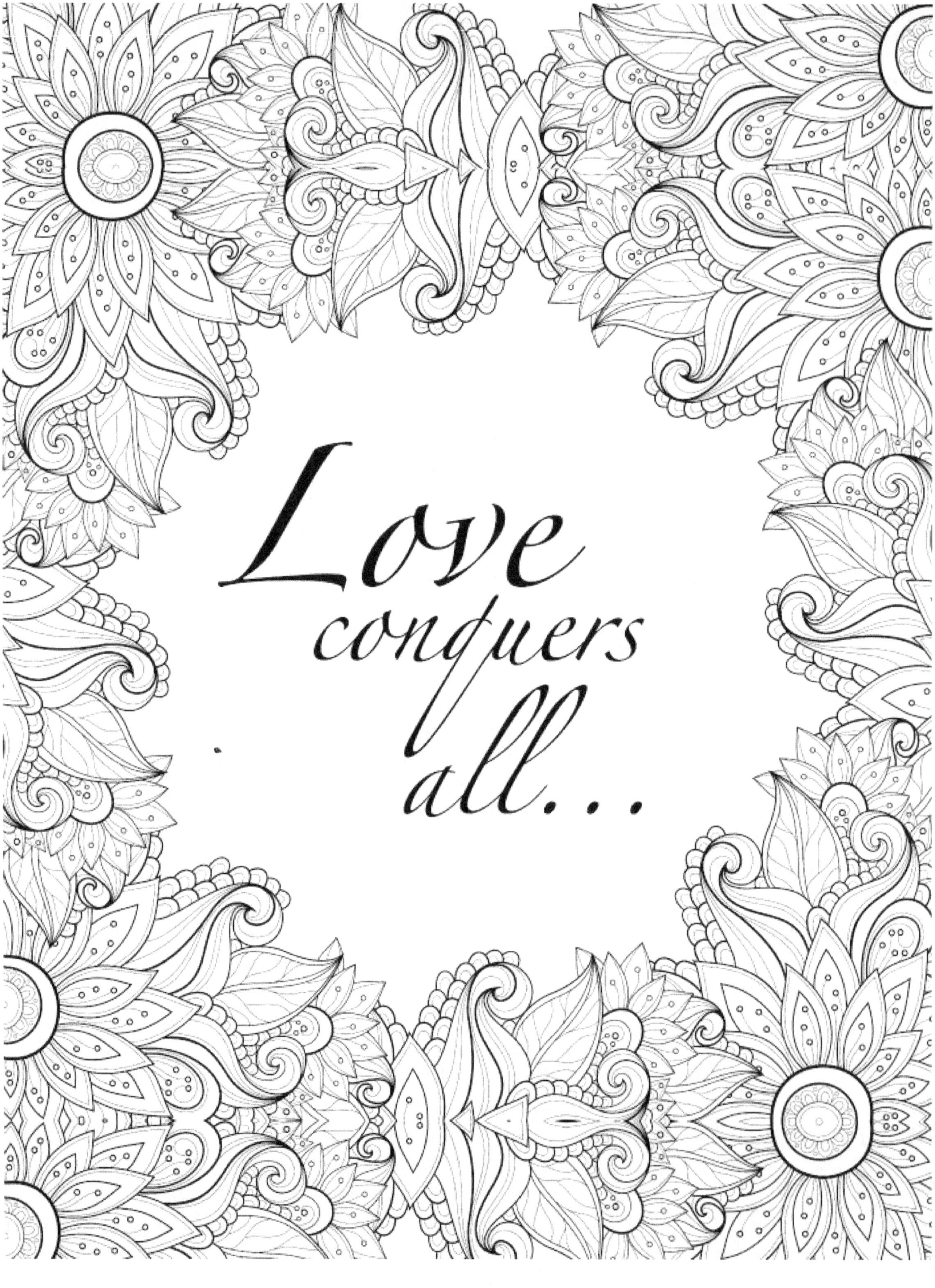
Love
conquers
all...

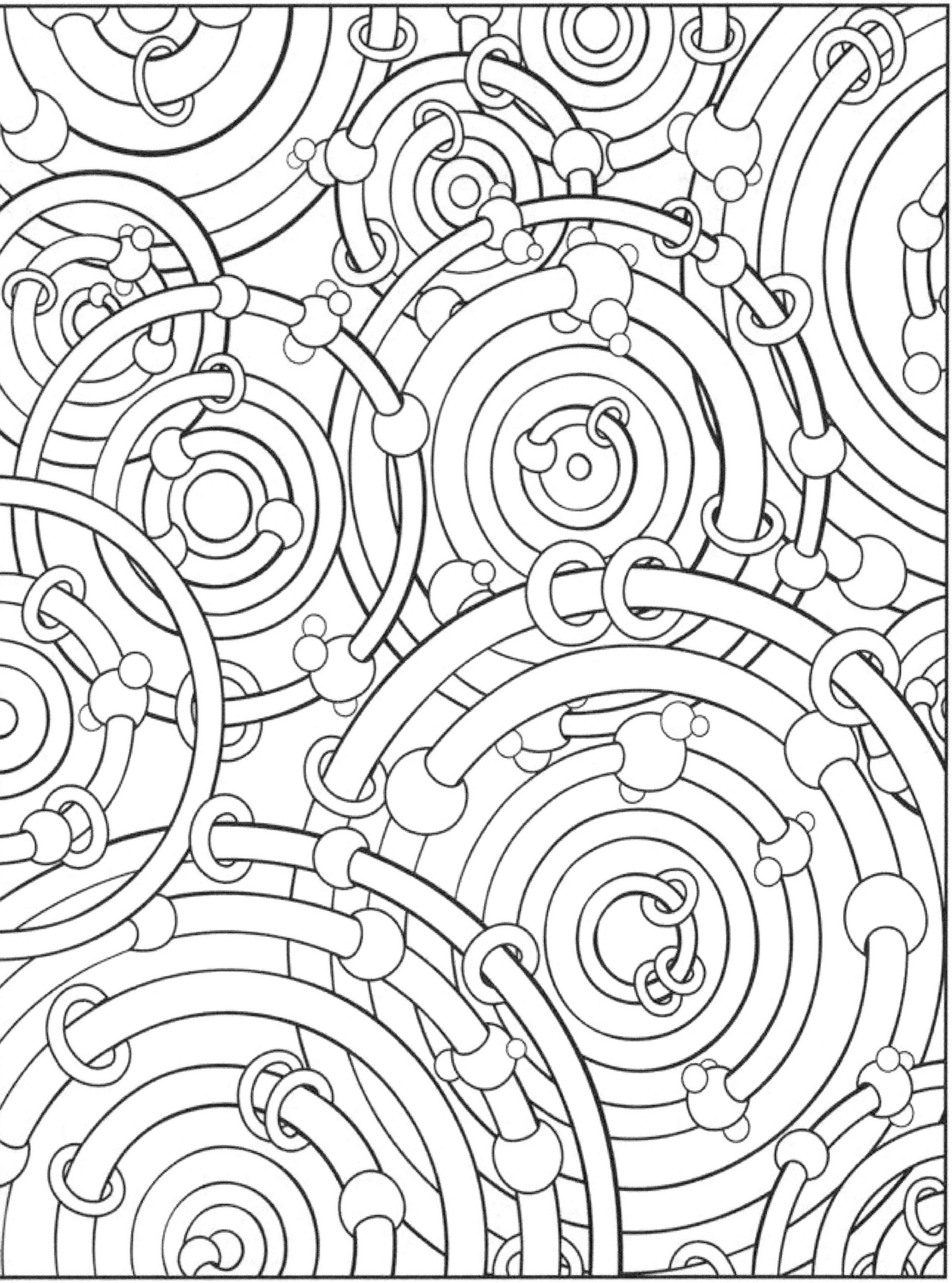

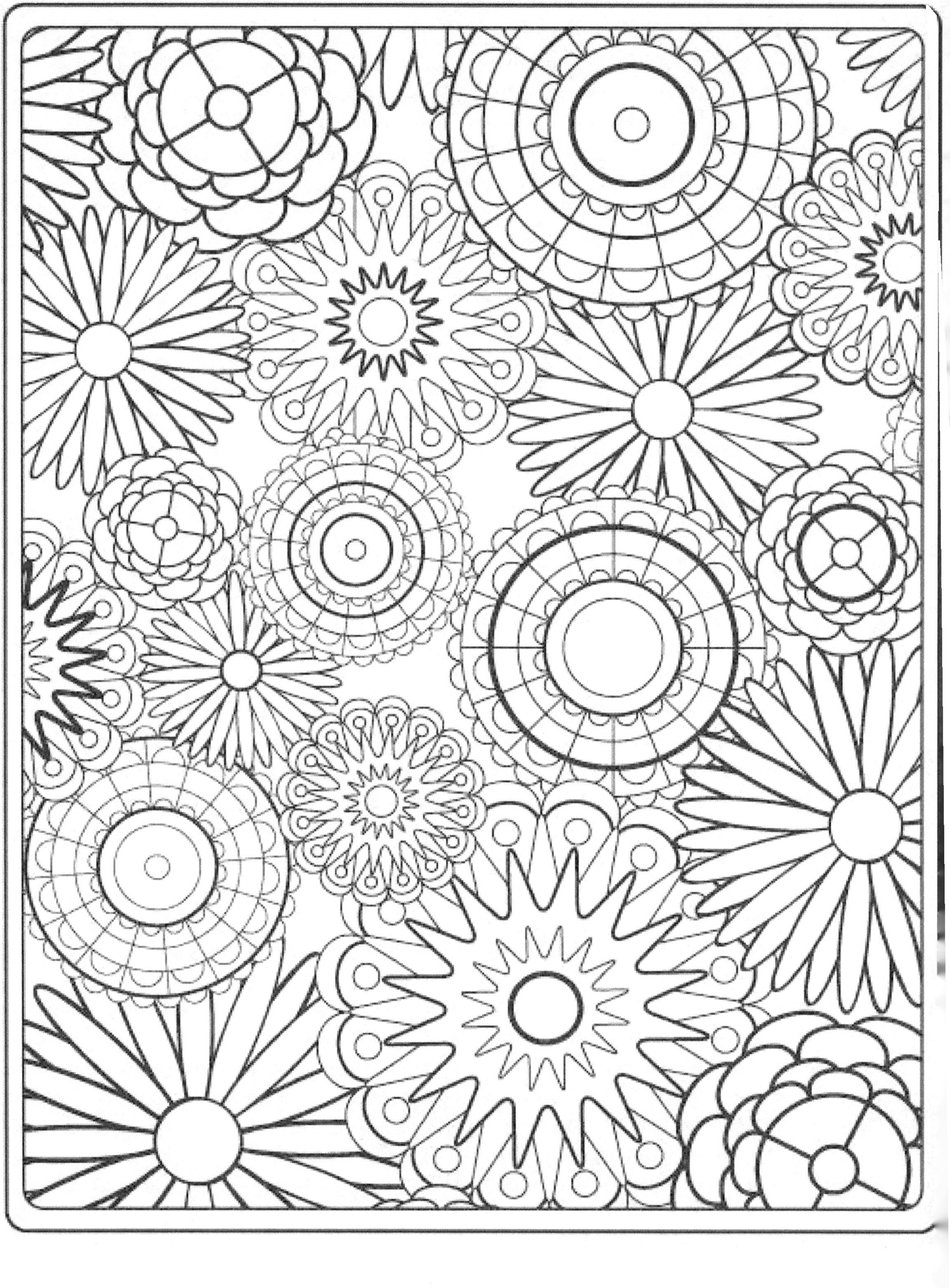

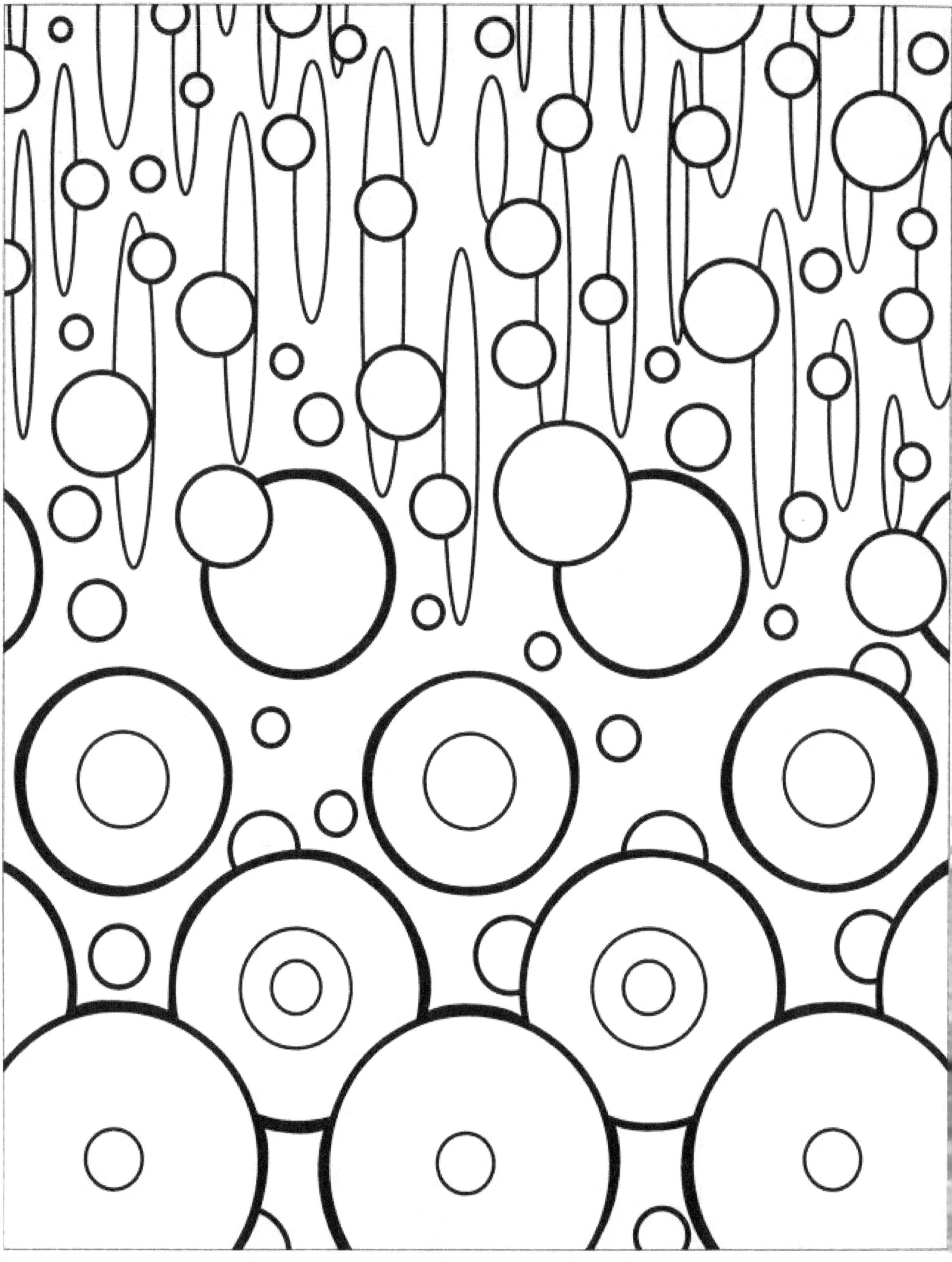

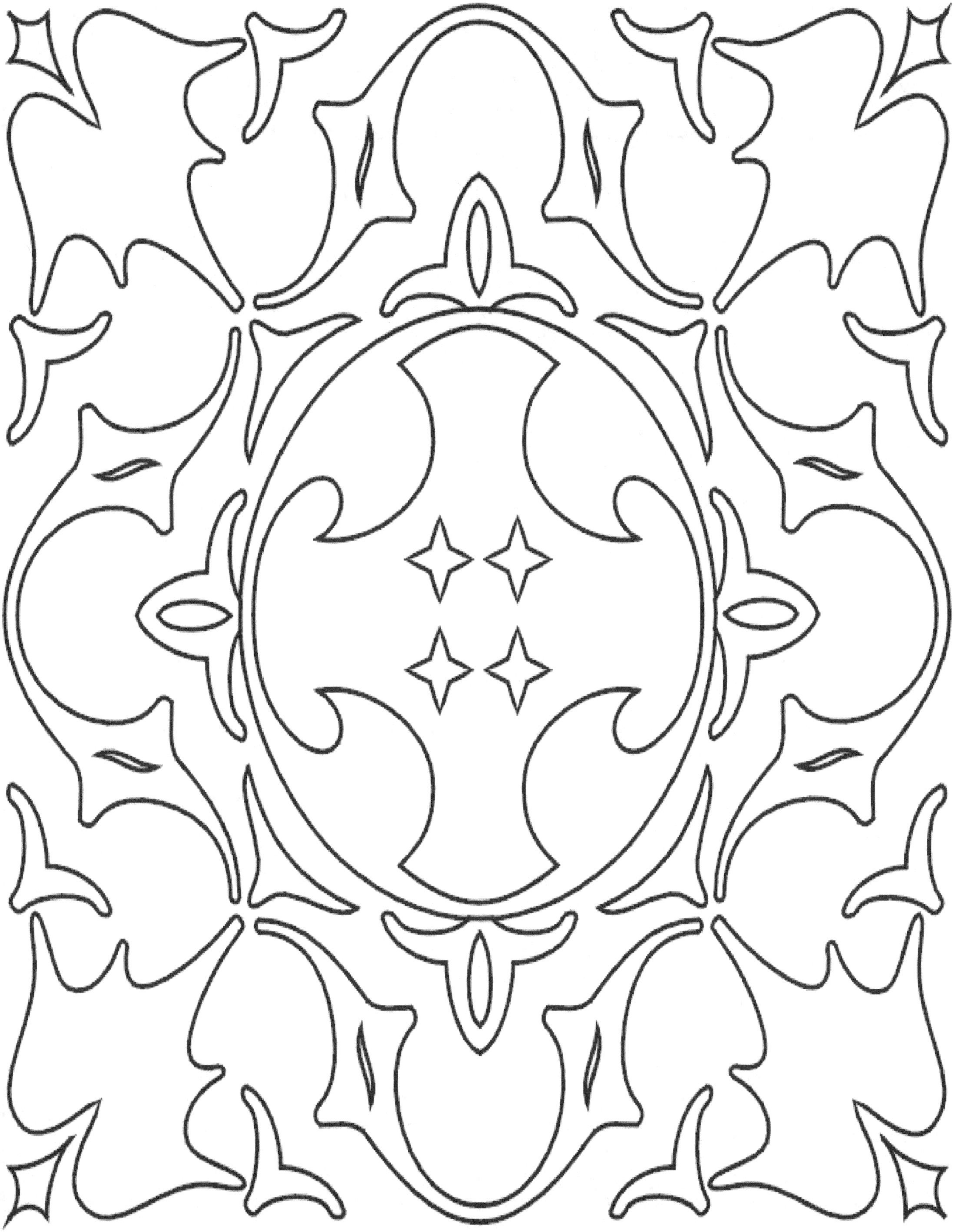

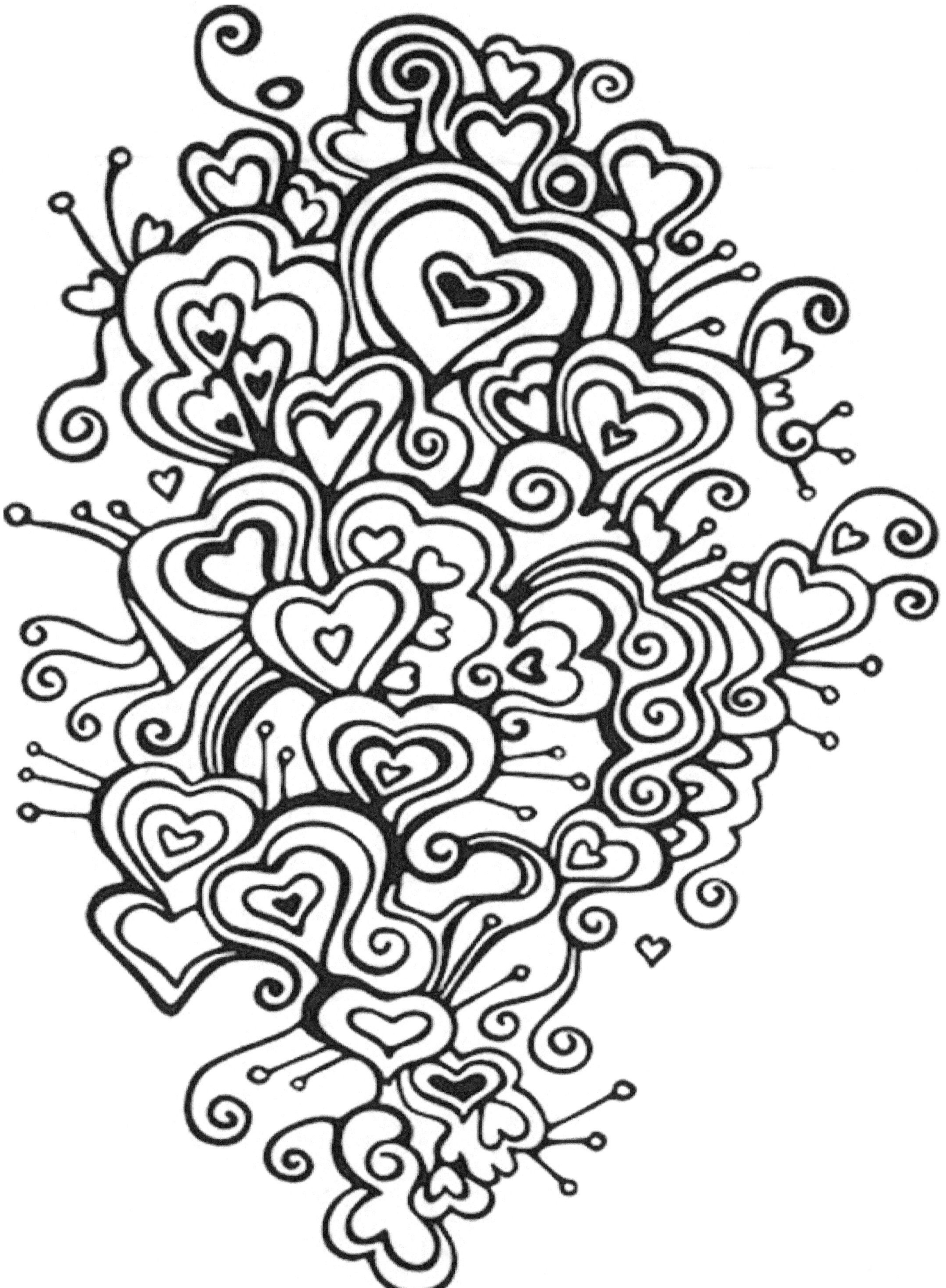

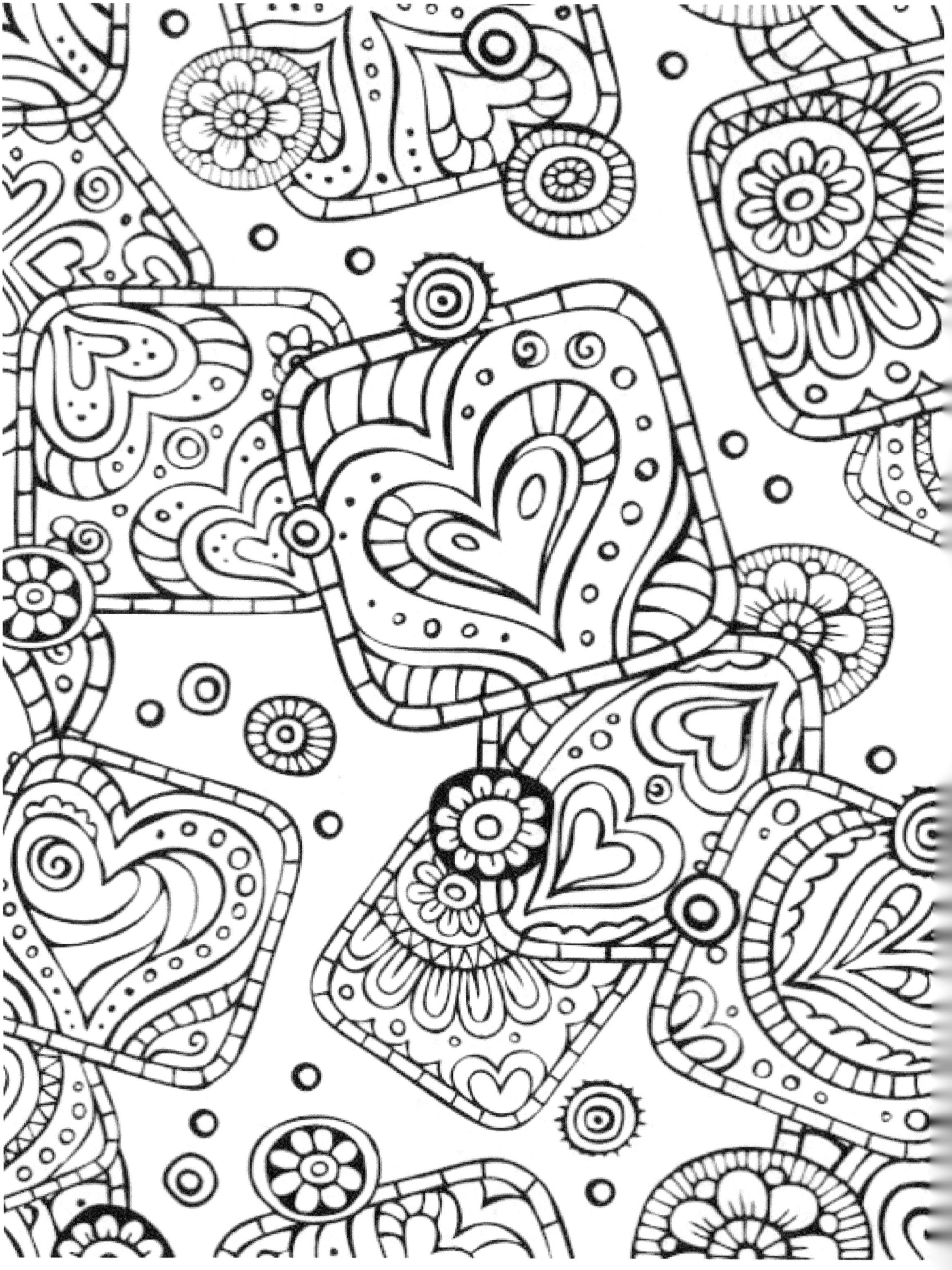

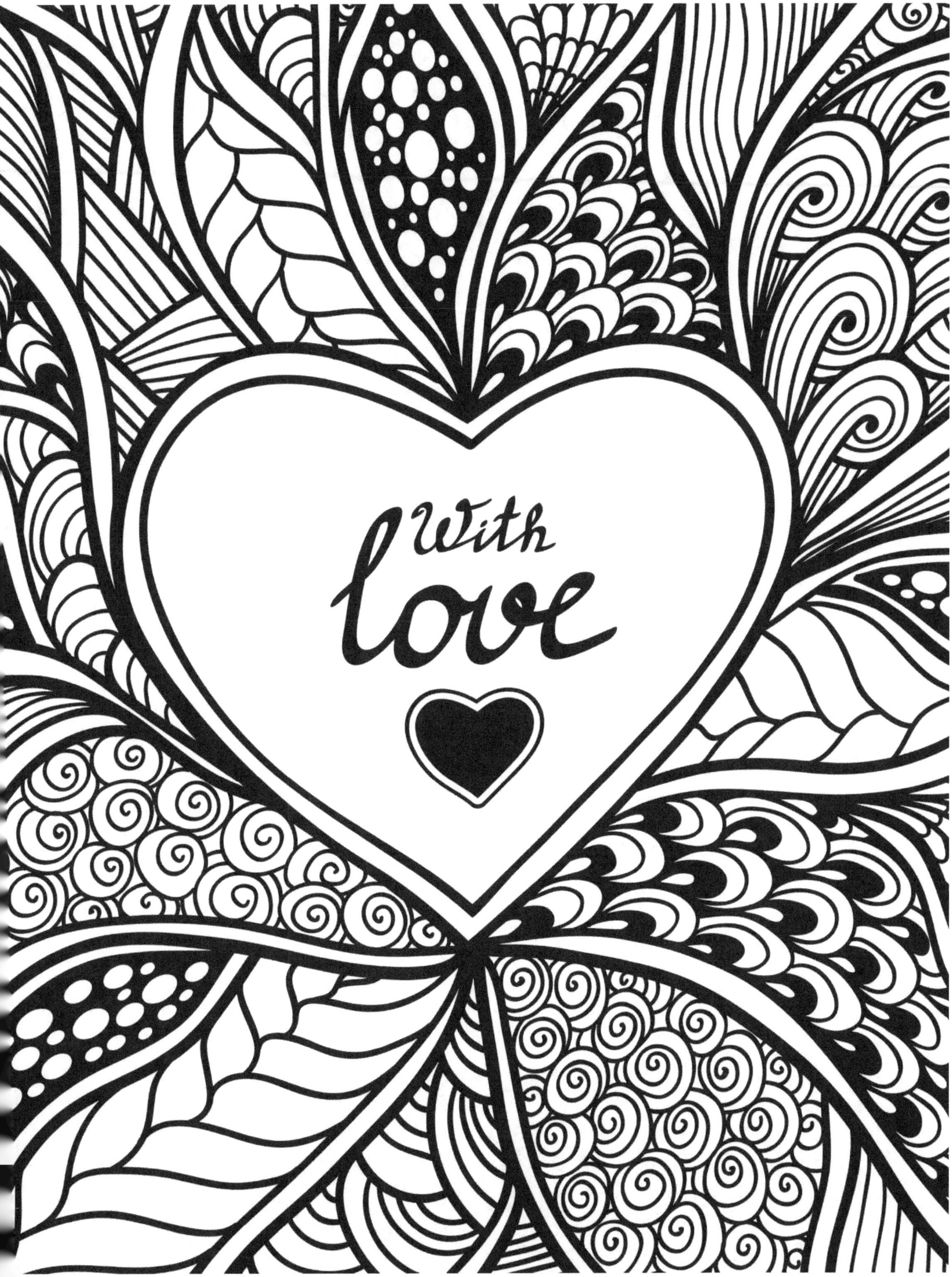
With love

www.ingramcontent.com/pod-product-compliance
Lightning Source LLC
Chambersburg PA
CBHW082148230526
45467CB00043B/2411
9798688365719